Previously Published by
THE FRIENDS OF THE UNIVERSITY OF TOLEDO LIBRARIES
Noel Stock
EZRA POUND'S PENNSYLVANIA
(1976)

Dorothy L. Sayers

WILKIE COLLINS
A CRITICAL AND BIOGRAPHICAL STUDY

Edited from the Manuscript
Humanities Research Center
Austin, Texas

by

E. R. Gregory

THE FRIENDS OF THE UNIVERSITY OF
TOLEDO LIBRARIES
1977

Text and previously unpublished writings
of Dorothy L. Sayers
©Anthony Fleming
Introduction ©E. R. Gregory

Library of Congress Cataloging in Publication Data

Sayers, Dorothy Leigh, 1893-1957.
  Dorothy L. Sayers' Wilkie Collins.

  Includes bibliographical references.
  1. Collins, Wilkie, 1824-1889. 2. Novelists, English—19th century—Biography. I. Title, II. Title: Wilkie Collins.
PR4497.S28   1977   823'.8 [B]   76-53108
ISBN 0-918160-01-4

PREFACE

I cannot claim to have discovered the ms. of Dorothy L. Sayers' Wilkie Collins, *because it was never really lost. I did, however, feel the thrill of discovery when, several summers ago, I happened on it in the Humanities Research Center, Austin, Texas. It was common knowledge that Miss Sayers had contemplated a biography of Collins at one time; but the amount of the work that she had completed was not widely known. It was also "common knowledge" that she had definitely abandoned the work at some point in her career, but, as I discovered, this "knowledge" was erroneous.*

Upon reading the ms., I was immediately struck with its importance. Despite its incomplete and unedited state, some of its perceptions were so just and so well-expressed that I felt it would be a genuine loss both to lovers of Sayers and of Collins were it to remain unpublished. Publishers were understandably reluctant to publish an incomplete work, but fortunately Leslie W. Sheridan, the Director of The University of Toledo Libraries, agreed with me as to the importance of publishing the ms. fragment. Thus, it makes its appearance under the aegis of the Friends of The University of Toledo Libraries.

Editing the ms. has been a major undertaking. In doing it, fortunately, I had the assistance of a number of institutions and of many, many persons. The University of Toledo generously supported my research with a number of grants, and the staffs of the Humanities Research Center and of Wheaton College, Illinois, were uniformly gracious.

I should also like to thank the following persons for their assistance: Richard D. Altick, Robert P. Ashley, Joe R. Christopher, Livia Gollancz, John F. Lehmann, Sue Lonoff, Wallace Martin, Barbara Reynolds, Kenneth Robinson, Timothy Scanlon, Noel Stock, and Alice O. Weaver.

Preface

The illustrations are the ones that Miss Sayers indicated that she wished to include. The sketch of Collins as a child is reproduced with the permission of its present owner, Douglas Ewing. In this edition, it is reproduced in color for the first time. The portrait of Collins by Holman Hunt is reproduced by permission of the National Portrait Gallery; the pages from the ms. of Basil, *by permission of the British Library. The playbill of* The Lighthouse *is reversed from a photostat in the Sayers Collection, Humanities Research Center. I preferred to use this for its associational value over a direct photograph of the playbill. The photographs of pages in* Antonina *and the* Memoirs of William Collins *were done by Roger Kennedy from copies in the University of Michigan Library.*

Finally, I must thank Anthony Fleming for permission to print the ms. and for the care with which he read my edition.

E. R. G.
Toledo, Ohio
September, 1977

INTRODUCTION

1. Dating

No other literary figure exercised so long-lasting an influence on Dorothy L. Sayers as Wilkie Collins. Before the publication of the first Lord Peter novel, *Whose Body?*, in 1923, she was already contemplating a biography; and only a few months before her death, she was still expressing the hope that someday she would get on with the work that she had never finished, yet never quite laid aside. The first reference to a projected biography is in a letter to her from the bookseller, Myles Radford, 15th June 1921: "When," he asked, "are you going to get your 'Life' published? I really think you ought to have it out shortly, and I feel sure you have as much information about Wilkie as is likely to come to light, and a great deal more than most 'Memoirs' contain."[1] If, in later years, Miss Sayers came across Radford's letter — and it remained in her files until she died — his question must have come with the passage of time to sound like cruel irony; for in July 1957, she wrote to T. I. F. Armstrong of "regrets that pressure of other business has prevented her from proceeding with the Biography of Wilkie Collins, although she still hopes to finish it, if and when old age brings leisure."[2] If and when .... A few months later she was dead.

Despite a documentable interest span of at least thirty-six years, however, "pressure of other business" telescoped a majority of her work on the biography into a few brief years in the late twenties and early thirties. The ms. fragment that we possess begins at the beginning with Collins' antecedents and proceeds, chapter by chapter, to November 1855. No reason exists to suppose that any sizable portion of the biography is missing, and it is therefore reasonable to conclude that she composed the chapters in sequential order. If this is true, she

---

[1] Letter in Humanities Research Center, Austin, Texas, referred to hereafter as H.R.C.
[2] Letter in H.R.C. The date, which is pencilled in, is not in Miss Sayers' handwriting, so we should note the possibility of error.

cannot have begun composition much before 1931, because the rough draft of Chapter I refers to Stewart M. Ellis' *Wilkie Collins, Le Fanu, and Others,* which was published in 1931.

Interestingly enough, Ellis' book is also the last-published work from which she quotes. As such, it forms a part of the tenuous evidence we must assess in establishing a *terminus ad quem* for the biography. In 1933, she was still sufficiently interested in the project to hire A. May Osler as a research assistant, and twenty-one letters from Osler to Sayers survive, dating from 18th February 1933 to 2d October 1933/34.

Thereafter, evidence of Sayers' interest in Collins thins out. On 20th February 1936, she writes to another bookseller, Raphael King, who had sent her the typescript of two Collins letters: "I have been terribly busy lately and unable to do any work on Collins, but some day I hope to be able to get to work on him again." Eight years later, she uses almost the same words in a letter to the American scholar, James Sandoe: "I am very glad to have these [copies of Collins letters], since I am always hoping some day to be able to get on with my life of him . . ." (6th January 1944).

The problem is complicated by the fact that she did other work on Collins in addition to her biography — the section on him in the *Cambridge Bibliography of English Literature* and the introduction to the Everyman Library edition of *The Moonstone.*[3] But did she do any further work on the biography after the early thirties? One other piece of evidence, admittedly inconclusive, exists. In 1948, Robert P. Ashley, who was himself working on a biography of Collins, wrote Sayers a number of queries about her research. She replied, 12th July 1948: "Dear Sir: If I were to put in about six weeks' intensive work on the material I laid aside fifteen years ago, I might be able to answer some of your questions fully; but I fear that

---

[3]The form letter from F. W. Bateson enclosing the galley proofs for her contribution to the *CBEL* is dated 5th August 1935. Everyman made its offer to her prior to February 1941, because its files contain a letter so dated from her agents — Pearn, Pollinger, and Higham — that confirms its offer to her for the introduction. Volume III of the *CBEL*, which contains her contribution, appeared in 1941; the introduction to *The Moonstone*, in June 1944. The form letter from Bateson is in the H.R.C.; the information about Everyman I got from its editorial manager, Jocelyn Burton, in a letter of 15th December 1976; the dates of publication, from Joe R. Christopher's "Dorothy Leigh Sayers: A Chronology," *Sayers Rev.*, I (Sept. 1976), 7, 9.

under present conditions I cannot find the time."[4] It is possible, of course, that she was using "fifteen years" in a general and imprecise way; but the biographical nature of the queries — did Collins have any children by Carolyn Graves, for example — and the neatness with which 1933 fits into the pattern of evidence suggest that she was writing with characteristic precision and that, in fact, she did little on the biography thereafter.

Printed assertions to the contrary, however, she never completely abandoned the idea. In his *Dickens,* Hesketh Pearson states quite unequivocally that "Miss Dorothy Sayers informed the present writer that it was 'the extreme obscurity which surrounds the whole of Collins' private life which discouraged me from getting on with the biography that I had contemplated.'"[5] The facts are less definite. On 9th March 1948, she had written to Kenneth Robinson, who was also doing research on Collins' life: "I will not say that I have altogether given up the idea of some time writing something about Wilkie Collins, but I have had to put off the scheme indefinitely, in favour of more urgent work, and there is nothing at all to prevent you from writing the biography you have in mind." Upon reading Pearson, Robinson wrote to Sayers again, assuming the information was correct and asking if he might see her Collins materials. She replied, 4th November 1949:

> I don't think I told Mr. Pearson quite that. I never "definitely abandon" anything. No doubt I shall one day have definitely to abandon life — but even then I shall probably [do] so with the greatest reluctance, protesting that there were still a great many things I had intended to do with it. All my Wilkie Collins stuff is at present stored away — but I mean to do something with it sometime if I can manage it, though it may not be exactly a biography (the fellow really had no "life" to speak of, had he?) but something more in the nature of a critical study.
>
> But if Atropos uses the shears before I get to that point, I will leave all the material to the nation, and then it will be available to everybody.[6]

The situation, then, seems to be this: she had modified her

---

[4]Letter in possession of Robert P. Ashley. Sayers does not seem to have saved either his letter or those of Kenneth Robinson mentioned below.

[5]*Dickens* (New York: Harper, 1949), p. 210.

[6]Letters in possession of Kenneth Robinson.

ideas of what she hoped to accomplish in writing about Collins, but she had not lost interest in him; and this the other facts, such as they are, confirm.

She probably continued to purchase books on Collins as they appeared;[7] she specifically stated to her friend, Barbara Reynolds, that she planned someday to finish her biography; and, finally, she wrote to T. I. F. Armstrong of "hopes to finish it, if and when old age brings leisure."

2. The Collinsean Influence on Sayers

What attracted Dorothy L. Sayers to Wilkie Collins in the first place, and why did she never completely abandon him? We can probably never ascertain the exact details of her introduction to Collins, but we can make some general observations that are suggestive. Robert P. Ashley has demonstrated that the reading public's esteem of Collins remained high through the nineties and the early years of the twentieth century.[8] Whatever else Collins' novels may be, the best of them are enthralling examples of the story-teller's art. Of *The Moonstone,* J. I. M. Stewart has written that "no English novel shows a structure and proportions, or contrives a narrative tempo, better adapted to its end: that of lending variety and amplitude to a story the mainspring of which has to be a sustained interest in the elucidation of a single mysterious event."[9] As we shall see shortly, Dorothy L. Sayers, even as a sophisticated and knowledgeable adult, continued to value highly the art of telling a story well. It is very likely, then, that the rectory at Bluntisham where she grew up contained some copies of Collins' works and that these works were precisely the kind of fare to engage the complete attention of a precocious, though as yet unsophisticated, child.

Her more careful, scholarly study of him formed a part of

---

[7]One wishes that greater certainty were possible on this point. The bookseller's catalogue of Sayers' Collins collection listed copies of Ashley's and Robinson's biographies as well as the later one of Nuel Pharr Davis. It did not in all respects correspond with the collection. In examining the copies of these books in the H.R.C., I found no tangible evidence (bookplate, signature, marginalia) to indicate that they had belonged to her. The most one can assert is that she *probably* bought these books. Ashley and Robinson are both definite that they did not send her copies.
[8]"Wilkie Collins Reconsidered," *NCF,* 4 (1950), 265-273.
[9]Introduction to *The Moonstone* (Harmondsworth, Eng.: Penguin, 1966), p. 7.

her preparation as a writer of detective stories; and his influence on her in this area was enormous, revealing itself in small details and fundamental attitudes alike. It is of little consequence that the name of Martha Ruddle in *Busman's Honeymoon* suggests Collins' mistress, Martha Rudd, but it is of great consequence that Sayers' feeling for what the detective story should be derived in large part from her reading of Collins, and it is of even greater importance that the attitudes engendered by that reading remained with her long after she turned from fiction to criticism and scholarship.

That Sayers, when she finally read Dante in the summer of 1944, preferred him to Collins is not surprising. The question of why she never quite abandoned Collins, however, remains. The fact of the matter is that her most interesting responses to Dante formed themselves round perceptions of Collins that she had earlier developed. Consider the following quotations:

> in order . . . to gain the reader's attention in the first place, and in order to secure his belief in far more astonishing parts of the narrative, the writer, if he knows his business, will strive for the utmost and most exact realism in the details of everything that happens "within the reader's own experience."
>
> if you want the reader not only to follow but to accept and believe a tale of marvels, you can do it best by the accumulation of precise and even prosaic detail.

The first statement refers to Collins; the second, to Dante.[10] Without context, no one could distinguish them.

A lifetime spent in academic circles might in some ways have been a better preparation for Sayers' work on Dante than her study of Collins and work as a novelist, but it could not have prepared her any better to appreciate "the accumulation of precise and even prosaic detail" as a strategy in Dantean art.

Collins' influence in sharpening her appreciation of this strategy co-exists, of course, with that of other writers whom she admired and with what she learned as a practicing novelist. His influence is nevertheless considerable. In her biography, she notes again and again his passion for factual accuracy:

---

[10] The first quotation appears in Chapter IV of the present work, pp. 82; the second, in Sayers' essay, " ' . . . And Telling you a Story': a Note on *The Divine Comedy*,"in *Essays presented to Charles Williams* (London: Oxford Univ. Press, 1947), p. 7.

> The passion for documentation, the confident appeal to historical fact, with which the sensation novelists of the century defended themselves against the charge of improbability are already present in the preface to *Antonina*. There are the accents of the same voice which in *Basil* protests: "I founded the main event out of which this story springs, on a fact within my own knowledge"; which called in "professional men" to witness the accuracy of the law, medicine and chemistry of *Armadale* . . . " (p. 67).

Thus, and much, much more.

The effect of this on her own fiction is obvious. Her detective stories are, in a sense, tales of marvels, although they do not appear as such on a first reading. In order to demonstrate how "marvelous" *The Nine Tailors* is, John G. Cawelti has had to lay out its plot sequentially. This done, one notes the "incredible tissue of improbability, coincidence, and turgid sensationalism" upon which the novel is built.[11] As he immediately goes on to say, however, this is not the impression it leaves; and although there are many reasons why it does not, high on any list must be "the accumulation of precise and even prosaic detail" by which Sayers has captured the reader's confidence. The notebooks, now at Wheaton College, Illinois, in which she worked out the technical aspects of change-ringing testify eloquently to the work that capture represents. As one examines page after page of mathematical formulae, one can only admire the energy and dedication with which she acquired the facts necessary to compel her readers "not only to follow but to accept and believe a tale of marvels . . . ."

Small wonder, then, that she exhorts the reader of the *Purgatory*

> to remember that he is at the Antipodes, and not to get his compass-points muddled up. Dante, though he had never in his life crossed the Line, has no moments of forgetfulness or confusion, which is more than can be said for most of us who live beneath the Wain. Readers in Australia, New Zealand, and South Africa will find that (for once, in a European literary classic) the Sun is in the right part of the sky.[12]

In short, the Collins biography confirms the growing impression among her admirers that underlying her work,

---

[11] *Adventure, Mystery, and Romance* (Chicago: Univ. of Chicago Press, 1976), p. 121.
[12] Introduction to *Purgatory* (Harmondsworth, Eng.: Penguin, 1955), p. 71.

despite its variety of expression, is the unity of a solid and enduring personality. A good story-teller herself, she prized both Collins and Dante as story-tellers, the possessors, she believed, of a gift that is innate and not acquired. Of this gift, she wrote that "it is mightiest in the mighty: by itself, it can produce the minor immortality of a *Sherlock Holmes* or a *Three Musketeers;* in the hands of a great poet it produces the major immortality of an *Odyssey,* a *Paradise Lost,* or a *Divine Comedy."* She was ready enough to admit that there was more to Dante than his ability to tell a story, but she always came back to assert "that the whole vast structure of Dante-study and Dante-criticism — theological, philosophical, historical, philological, poetical and what-not — beneath which the bookshelves of Christendom sag, is carried upon the sturdy bones of a narrative . . . ."[13] When every qualification has been made, the fact is that her study of Collins made her a better novelist and a better critic. Willing enough to grant his limitations, she nevertheless appraised him fairly. We have no reason to think that she valued him less highly in 1957 than she did in 1921.

3. Value as Collins Scholarship

All of the above is of interest to Sayers' admirers, but the work that follows is also of interest to Collins'. To be sure, it is in some respects obsolete now. At the beginning of Chapter II, for example, Sayers speculates at length on when and where Collins attended school without coming to any definite conclusion. On those matters, the facts now are in. They are revealed in the Collins letters, formerly in the possession of A. P. Watt, now in the Pierpont Morgan Library. These letters Robinson used extensively in preparing his biography, where he states the facts succinctly: before the Italian journey, young Wilkie attended the Maida Hill Academy; afterwards, he attended a private school in Highbury run by a Mr. Cole.[14]

In other respects, the biography needs to be supplemented

---

[13]"The Eighth Bolgia," in *Further Papers on Dante* (London: Methuen, 1957), p. 102.
[14] *Wilkie Collins* (New York: Macmillan, 1952), pp. 24, 29. The letters in the Morgan, which are uncatalogued, I have not examined. Robinson has stated that the Watt file was the source of his information, and my colleague Sue Lonoff has partially verified this. The file definitely contains a number of letters from Collins written while at Mr. Cole's school in Highbury. These post-date the Italian journey and include two to his mother, written in Italian and headed "Piazza di Highbury"!

by subsequent scholarship. Sayers' discussion of *Basil* in Chapter IV is full and penetrating, but it needs Nuel Pharr Davis' observations about source material to complete it. The parallels that Davis cites between Basil and Philip Stanhope are convincing as is his evidence that the Dickens circle was most interested in the Stanhope family and particularly in the Earl of Chesterfield's dealings with the forger, William Dodd.[15]

On the whole, however, the biography stands up very well indeed. To aid in her research, Sayers assembled an impressive ms. collection, some of which is printed in the following pages for the first time. The most important of the mss. on which she draws is the "Reminiscences of a Story-Teller" quoted in Chapter II, for the version published in the *Universal Review* (1888) was considerably altered. All of this material is now in the H. R. C.; and wherever she refers to it, I note that fact.

Finally, despite evidence that she composed hastily, Sayers' combination of liveliness and scholarship provides a still-illuminating commentary on Collins. Consider her opening paragraph:

> William Wilkie Collins was a typical Englishman: that is to say, he was born in London of a Scotch mother and a Scotch-Irish father of English ancestry, lived all his sixty-five years in and around the parish of Marylebone; and took every opportunity of disparaging all the countries of his origin in favour of France. He possessed the English sentimentality with the English insensitiveness of taste; the English exuberance of imagination with the English matter-of-fact business ability; the vague English leaning towards theoretical democracy with the practical English tact in the handling of social distinctions; the English championship of Woman with the English hatred of learned women; and that peculiar English genius for combining melodrama with calculation which has made the English detective story a thing apart.

Seldom has so much information been condensed into so brief a space, and with such elegance of phrasing. And who else but Miss Sayers could make reading about *Antonina* a positive pleasure? As she sums up on p. 66, she manages the difficult feat of being both accurate and amusing: "The historical facts are there, but not the historical sense; Goths and Romans alike hail from Wardour Street; the fifth-century Christians are

---

[15]*Life of Wilkie Collins* (Urbana: Univ. of Ill. Press, 1956), pp. 116-117.

nineteenth-century Protestants; the stock villain, virgin, and fanatic utter the stock sentiments appropriate to villainy, virginity, and fanaticism." So much for *Antonina*.

In addition to elegance of expression, the biography also reveals an ability to separate the wheat from the chaff where a lesser individual would have been overwhelmed by the sheer quantity of chaff. It is easy enough to ridicule *Antonina;* it is more difficult to make a convincing case, as she does, that in it "faint and gasping beneath the historical trappings, the author of *The Women in White* is struggling into view" (p. 67).

4. The Manuscript and Compositional Habits

After Sayers' death, the ms. of the biography, her notecards, notebooks (with one exception), correspondence on Collins, and the mss. of Collins and books by and about him that she had collected were put together to form a collection for sale. The one exception is a notebook in the Wade Collection at Wheaton College. It was separated from the other Collins materials because it also contained ms. versions of some of the Lord Peter stories. It is of the same manufacture as one of the notebooks in the H. R. C., so Sayers probably purchased and worked on them at about the same time. A Lord Peter story in the notebook, "The Fantastic Horror of the Cat in the Bag," had been written by November 1927, because Sayers discussed its publication with Gollancz at that time.[16] With regard to Collins, the notebook contains a list of Collins' letters by year, a list of books and articles about Collins, a list of Collins' obituaries, and a list of his articles in *Household Words* and *All the Year Round*. Since the first entry in the list of books and articles is the Oxford University Press's edition of *The Moonstone,* which was published in 1928, we can assume that she worked on this material in 1927-28.

Since the H. R. C. does not open its files to scholars, the following must be taken as its official statement of how it acquired the Sayers collection of Collinseana:

> The Dorothy Sayers collection was first brought to our

---

[16]It was one of nine stories that later formed part of the collection published as *Lord Peter Views the Body* (letter from Livia Gollancz, 7th September 1976).

attention during the summer of 1960 by Mr. Lew David Feldman (House of El Dieff, New York). The collection of manuscripts, books, and related materials was at that time the property of Mr. Anthony Fleming, son of the late Dr. Sayers. Acting as Fleming's agent was Mr. Robert Barry, Jr. (C. A. Stonehill, Inc., New Haven). A twenty-page list of the materials was made available for our consideration. It was mentioned that the collection being offered at the time did not represent the complete manuscript and book holdings of the Estate.

On 28 October 1960, we ordered the Sayers collection through Mr. Feldman. In July, 1961, we received word that Mr. Barry had received the materials, had carefully checked them against the list provided, and was shipping them directly to Texas. Barry mentioned that the list was not completely accurate — a few items were not included in the collection, although there were some materials present which had not been listed. The materials arrived here on 3 August 1961.[17]

A catalogue of the materials involved in the purchase is available from the H. R. C. Their discussion for the most part falls outside the scope of this introduction, although I would note that two tentative tables of contents do exist. One projects twenty-two chapters for the complete work; the other, nineteen. These do not, unfortunately, help much in determining the percentage of the work envisaged that we have because the chapter headings do not fit with the chapters completed.

The ms. itself consists of four completed chapters and a substantial section of a fifth one. The first chapter exists in three states — a rough draft comparable to the state of the other chapters; a fair copy that Sayers prepared for a professional typist; and a typed copy. If one counts the pages of the rough draft of Chapter I, one has approximately 141 pages of ms. Between the chapters, she inserted sheets of paper on which she indicated the visual materials that she wanted to include.

A close look at the ms. suggests that it was composed hastily. Although it contains a fair amount of authorial revision, many sentences were left incomplete or incompletely revised. For example, the date was left blank in the following sentence on p. 53, "Finally, they reached home on _____ , having been abroad almost two years, and missed, incidentally, the Queen's Coronation and the

---

[17]Letter from Ellen S. Dunlap, Research Librarian, H.R.C., 11th November 1976.

greater part of the *Pickwick Papers.*" And this despite the fact that the date, 15th August 1838, is given on one of the very pages in the *Memoirs of the Life of William Collins* from which she had just quoted.[18] Further evidence of haste in the same passage includes her spelling of "Innspruck" and "Salzburg." The "Innspruck" is a probably unconscious recollection of Collins' spelling in the *Memoirs.* Had she consciously tried to reproduce Collins' spelling, she would have spelled Salzburg "Saltzburg."

Incomplete revisions include such puzzles as the following:

> He was a boarder in the school—& this is quite natural, when
> at that,
> we consider that his home was at Bayswater, ~~surely~~ in the days
> & the L.G.O.C.
> before Underground ~~railways~~s, the distance between these two
> much too long a
> points would have been ~~a considerable~~ journey for a small boy to
> undertake daily.
>
> (Page 45)

> the central history of Basil's love-affair & its abominable
> ?little
> ending is told with a kind of grim actuality which has no relation
> to anything in comtemporary English fiction.
>
> (Page 86)

The point is not that Sayers was a slovenly workman, but rather that the ms. helps us to understand the kind of workman she was. Her practice seems to have been to block in the large outlines, then polish and fill in detail later. Unfortunately, she never got around to dotting her i's and crossing her t's in this particular ms. The result is a work that is unfinished both in the sense of being incomplete and the Horatian sense of not worked over for nine years.

5. Editorial Principles

Since the ms. gives evidence of having been worked on hastily, one must make any deductions about Miss Sayers' preferences with care, using other evidence wherever possible. Where inconsistencies were involved, my practice was to leave

---

[18] *Memoirs of the Life of William Collins* (London: Longman, Brown, Green, and Longmans, 1848), II, 154.

them unless they might interfere with the reader's convenience. Thus, Sayers sometimes placed commas and periods inside quotation marks in the approved American fashion, sometimes outside in the approved British fashion, and sometimes directly beneath the quotation mark in the fashion approved by freshmen the world over. The introductions in the Penguin edition of *The Divine Comedy,* which she carefully supervised, suggest that this particular matter did not greatly concern her. On page 20 of her introduction to the *Purgatory,* one finds "Spirits elect", "spirits formed for bliss". Opposite, on page 21, however, one finds the following:

> As, in C.S. Lewis' book, the devil Screwtape angrily explains to Wormwood, "they *embrace* those pains; they would not barter them for any earthly pleasure."

I have therefore left her punctuation as is except where intention was unclear, where I placed comma and period outside the quotation mark on the ground that this being standard British usage, the chances of her preferring it were slightly greater.

Similarly with dates. In her text, she will use the British and continental style in one paragraph — 8th January 1824 — and the American in the next—January 25th 1828 (p. 37). In her footnotes, however, she consistently uses the British style, complicating matters by an exclusive use of numbers — 11. 2. 86, for example. In each case, I have given the date as she gave it except in the notes, which I expanded for clarity's sake — 11th February 1886 in the instance given.

In punctuation and mechanics, Sayers' preferences were an interesting blend of the conservative and the individual. Although she had great respect for Fowler, she did not hesitate to part company from him when she cared to. In his entry on *today, tomorrow, tonight,* for example, Fowler wrote: "The lingering of the hyphen, which is still usual after the *to* of these words, is a very singular piece of conservatism;"[19] yet this was Sayers' consistent practice.

Perhaps her most notorious piece of individualism in these matters was her preference for the double quotation mark.

---

[19] *A Dictionary of Modern English Usage* (Oxford: Clarendon Press, 1926).

Indeed, she got sufficiently exercised over the matter when working on *The Divine Comedy* to write a little quatrain about it:

> And now I tune my brazen throat
> To sing in harsh, emphatic strain
> With what abhorrence, rage and pain
> I contemplate the SINGLE QUOTE.

Yet even here perhaps Sayers agreed with Emerson about a foolish consistency. In Chapter III, note 14, I believe that she consciously enclosed a quotation from Collins in single quotes to convey to the reader Collins' use, perhaps over-use, of quotation marks for effect. 'By this plan, it was thought . . . that, in the painter's phrase, the "effects" might thus be best "massed," and the "lights and shadows" most harmoniously "balanced" and "discriminated." '

A number of non-standard usages and spellings reflect the source that she was using. Forms like "New-Cavendish-street" and "Oxford-terrace" reflect Collins' usage in the *Memoirs of William Collins,* and indeed this is a frequently encountered form in nineteenth-century printing. The obituaries for Collins' death yield a number of examples. Similarly, Collins' *Memoirs* are the source of such strange spellings as "Sienna" and "Innspruck." Although I have kept these spellings, I note that in reproducing French names, she did not follow Collins, but used the French forms with which she was familiar. For the rest, her practice is not consistent enough to draw any conclusions.

More difficult to deal with because more substantive are the incomplete revisions quoted in the preceding section. In the first sentence quoted on p. 17, changing the "at" in "at that" to "and" seemed the most sensible emendation. The second sentence presented even more of a puzzle. Scholarly caution mandated the use of "little" rather than "no," and yet Sayers liked the boldly unqualified sentence. In the first instance, I had the advice of Barbara Reynolds, who probably knows more about the characteristic shape of the Sayersian sentence than anyone else; in the second, that of Richard D. Altick, who is similarly knowledgeable about mid-nineteenth century fiction. In neither instance am I certain that I fulfilled Sayers' wishes, and yet decisions had to be made. Each page offered puzzles of this nature; and although I could have bracketed each change that I made, the result in my view would have been the kind of arid pedantry that Sayers particularly detested. The reader can rest assured that I changed only what had to be changed in order to make an intelligible text.

The notes presented additional problems. As they exist in the ms., they are not so much formal references as they are memoranda to the author. Sayers cited not the editions that she used, but the editions she intended to use; she left notes to herself to verify information; she indicated intentions never carried out with phrases like "see appendix" and "v. subt. p. __." Though all such matters would be of interest to a small group of scholars, I felt that most readers would find their inclusion distracting and therefore omitted them.

The full citations that she gives make clear — as one would have surmised — that in the early period of Collins' life, she wished to use first editions. Since, in most instances, she did not have a first edition handy, she used the edition she had, planning doubtless on coming back and harmonizing her quotations with the intended edition at a later date. Thus, with regard to *Antonina,* she clearly indicated that she wished to use the first edition — *"Antonina; or, The Fall of Rome.* A Romance of the Fifth Century. By W. Wilkie Collins, author of the Life of William Collins, R. A. London: Richard Bentley, MDCCCL. 3 vols." Just as clearly, she quoted from a later edition. One could guess that she was working from an edition of *Antonina* other than the first from her description of its pages as "closely-printed and rhetorical" (p. 64). Rhetorical its pages certainly are, but no one could describe its well-spaced type as "closely-printed." Definitive proof, however, is provided by the chapter headings. In the three-volume edition, each volume was subdivided into books and chapters, whereas subsequent editions numbered chapters consecutively. Thus she ascribes the quotation on p. 64 — "Darkness had no obscurity that forced him to repose, and lassitude no eloquence that lured him to delay" — to Chapter 8, an ascription that fits other editions perfectly. If we return to the first edition, however, the ascription, according to chapter, should read as follows: vol. II, shed heavy darkness on the earth. Dense, stagnant vapours clung to the mountain summits; from the drooping trees dead leaves and rotten branches sunk, at intervals, on the oozy soil, or whirled over the gloomy precipice; and a small, steady rain fell, slow and unintermitting, upon the deserts around. Standing upon the path which armies had once trodden, and which armies were still destined to tread, and looking towards the solitary lake, you heard, at first, no sound but the regular dripping of the rain-drops from rock to rock; you saw no prospect but the motionless waters at your feet, and the dusky crags which shadowed them from above. When, however, impressed by the mysterious loneliness of the place, the eye grew more penetrating, and the ear more attentive, a cavern became apparent in the precipices round the lake; and, in the intervals of the heavy rain-drops, were faintly perceptible the sounds of a human voice.

The mouth of the cavern was partly concealed by a large stone, on which were piled some masses of rotten brushwood, as if for the purpose of pro-

Pages from First Edition of *Antonina*

Book First, Chapter I. Since this was ungainly, I simply cited volume and page number for the first edition.

For purposes of this project, I have not thought it necessary to identify the specific editions of Collins that Sayers used. Since her intentions were clear, I have quoted directly from the texts specified, going with them where they varied from her ms. In a few instances this created problems that called either for a footnote or a slight alteration in Miss Sayers' ms. In the first edition of *Basil,* Basil's older brother, Ralph, refers to his mistress as "Madame," whereas in the second and following editions, he refers to her as "Mrs. Ralph" and "the morganatic Mrs. Ralph." Since the quotations on p. 89 contain no reference to "the morganatic Mrs. Ralph," I either had to alter Sayers' summarizing sentence — "This has the authentic touch of nature, with its sly reference to the age of 'the morganatic Mrs. Ralph' and its rallying but not unfeeling amusement at the younger brother's helpless innocence" — or put in a footnote; and since I altered Sayers' words only with reluctance, in this instance I chose to put in the footnote.

In another instance, avoidance of pedantry necessitated the insertion of an extra sentence in the text. In the first edition of *Hide and Seek,* Collins introduces a number of visitors at Mr. Blyth's exhibition with the phrases, "there were" and "there was": "There were M. Bullivant, the sculptor, and Mr. Hemlock, the journalist .... There was Mr. Gimble, fluently laudatory ...." In the second and later editions, Collins altered these to the terser "also": "Also, Mr. Bullivant, the sculptor, and Mr. Hemlock, the journalist .... Also, Mr. Gimble, fluently laudatory ...." Sayers runs her quotation from the second edition into her text in the following way: "we are perfectly familiar with the 'two Royal Academicians," etc. Thus, the long series of *alsos* follow along easily, but "there were" and "there was" do not. I could have solved the problem by substituting ellipses for these phrases and bracketing in the word, *also,* each time it appeared; but considering the number of times involved, this seemed too great a strain to impose on the reader. I therefore inserted a sentence of my own on page 103 — "We also recognize the other types present" — after which the phrasing of the first edition follows easily.

The notes also offered a means for correcting and augmenting the text. Although Sayers was often imprecise in details, she made few outright errors. There are some. In Chapter V, for instance, she confuses the itinerary of the Italian journey. Dickens, Collins, and Egg went from Rome to Florence to Venice, whereas she has them go from Rome to Venice to Florence. This I correct in note 7.

Some of the augmentation is clearly in keeping with Sayers' wishes; some may not be. If we take Chapter I as our standard — and it is the most carefully worked on — she obviously did not expect her readers to know much, for she identifies Miss Clack as a character in *The Moonstone* and Zachary Thorpe as a character in *Hide and Seek*. It is reasonable to suppose then that she would have identified Mrs. Plornish, Little Billee, the Signora Neroni, and other characters from Victorian fiction. It is difficult, of course, to know where to draw the line. In Chapter I, she does not identify Captain Shandon, a character in *Pendennis,* though she could have little reason to think her audience would know him, and not Miss Clack. On the whole, I have preferred to err in the direction of inclusiveness. Thus, I have identified many sources that she did not, translated French passages into English, and so on. Even in the translating of French, I am not certain that I violate her wishes. Working in 1931, she may well have felt that persons ignorant of French had no business reading her scholarly works. Could one summon up her shade in these our decadent seventies, it might well murmur, "Autres temps, autres moeurs."

In addition to such changes as I have noted, I have made numerous ones in the interest of editorial consistency. Thus, the first note in Chapter I appears in the ms. as follows: *"Memoirs:* I, 4." This I expand to the following: *"Memoirs of the Life of William Collins, Esq., R. A.* (London: Longman, Brown, Green, and Longmans, 1848), I, 4." Independent though she was, Sayers was prepared to submit to a certain amount of tinkering of this nature, provided that no principles were involved. Such changes I do not indicate.

Wherever I thought her practice might have significance, however slight, I retained it. Thus, I placed the footnote numbers in the text where she placed them and not, as current practice dictates, at the end of phrases and sentences. Thus, too, I reproduce the full citations to the editions that she intended to use, as for example the citation to *Antonina* that I have quoted.

Substantive departures from Sayers' notes I indicate with special brackets, [[ ]], and, where needed, the abbreviation, *Ed*. The second note in Chapter I, for example, appears in the ms. thus: "Published 17___." Since Sayers owned a copy of the book referred to, *Memoirs of a Picture,* and since the book was only published once, little doubt can exist that she would have corrected the entry to the year of publication, 1805. Even with so obvious an example as this, however, one has left the realm of the demonstrable for speculation; and it has therefore seemed the better part of scholarly valor to note all such changes.

For the first chapter, it was a temptation to take the typescript as my text, but it was a temptation to be resisted. The typist was not careful in reproducing details of the ms. and in one instance, at least, created a full-fledged bibliographic ghost, the Reverend Carmo Wilson, whom reference to Sayers' script reveals to be merely that familiar bogey-man of Bronte biography, the Reverend Carus Wilson. I therefore used the intermediate version prepared for the typist as most nearly representing Sayers' final intention.

CHAPTER I
1824-1836

Origins of the Collins family — Old William Collins, the picture-dealer — *Memoirs of a Picture* — George Morland — William Collins the Painter — Early struggles — An R. A. at last — Marriage to Harriet Geddes — Birth of William Wilkie Collins — Hampstead — Birth of Charles Allston Collins — Family life of the Collinses — Mrs. Collins — Letter from a father to his sons — Sabbatarianism — Deaths of Mrs. Collins senior and Francis Collins — Departure for Italy.

WILLIAM WILKIE COLLINS was a typical Englishman: that is to say, he was born in London of a Scotch mother and a Scotch-Irish father of English ancestry, lived all his sixty-five years in and around the parish of Marylebone; and took every opportunity of disparaging all the countries of his origin in favour of France. He possessed the English sentimentality with the English insensitiveness of taste; the English exuberance of imagination with the English matter-of-fact business ability; the vague English leaning towards theoretical democracy with the practical English tact in the handling of social distinctions; the English championship of Woman with the English hatred of learned women; and that peculiar English genius for combining melodrama with calculation which has made the English detective story a thing apart.

His own account[1] of his ancestry is not a very full one. He has preserved a "favourite tradition" of his family that they came of the same stock as William Collins the poet, and mentions that they were directly descended from Dr. Samuel Collins, the seventeenth-century anatomist. We may, if we please, trace back Wilkie's medical and literary interests to these remote sources. But with his grandfather, William Collins the elder, we come to a very real influence, and to a character who deserves a little mention for his own sake.

---

[1] *Memoirs of the Life of William Collins, Esq., R.A.* (London: Longman, Brown, Green, and Longmans, 1848), I, 4.

Frontispiece and Title Page of *Memoirs of William Collins, R.A.*

Wilkie calls his grandfather "an Irishman, born in Wicklow." But he adds that "the family originally came from Chichester, whence, about the time of the Revolution of 1688, a branch of it emigrated to Ireland, and fought on the side of King William, at the Battle of the Boyne; settling definitely in Ireland from that period to the birth of" the elder William (*Memoirs*, I, 4). So that, County Wicklow or no County Wicklow, the Collinses were English on the male side, or, at the most, Orange-Irish. They were apparently well-to-do at the time of the Irish Settlement, but the Collins of the next generation indulged in "an imprudent marriage, bringing with it the usual train of domestic privations and disappointments", so that Grandfather William "found himself, on arriving at manhood, entirely dependent on his own exertions for support" (*Memoirs*, I, 4-5). Imprudent alliances seem to have run in the Collins family. William promptly handicapped himself with a young and portionless Scottish wife, and came over to make his fortune in London as a picture-dealer and a man of letters.

The elder William was, indeed, a perfect specimen of the crank journalist of his time — lovable, versatile and hopelessly unbusiness-like. He belonged to a period when: —

> the fine old race of genuine *garret* authors still existed, to fire the ingenuity of rapacious bailiffs, and point the sarcasms of indignant biographers. Articles in the public journals, songs, fugitive pieces, and all the other miscellanies of the literary brain, flowed plentifully from Mr. Collins's pen; gaining for him the reputation of a smart public writer, and procuring for him an immediate, but scanty support. No literary occupations were too various for the thoroughly Irish universality of his capacity. He wrote sermons for a cathedral dignitary, who was possessed of more spiritual grace then intellectual power; and, during the administration of Mr. Wyndham, composed a political pamphlet, to further the views of a friend; which procured that fortunate individual a Government situation of four hundred a year, but left the builder of his fortunes in the same condition of pecuniary embarrassment in which he had produced the pamphlet, and in which, to the last day of his life, he was fated to remain.
> (*Memoirs*, I, 6-7)

So writes Wilkie; and if the style is a little stilted, the portrait is typical. Old William Collins was of the race of Captain Shandon and Wilkins Micawber — always in difficulties and always undefeated. His journalism brought him into contact with all the leading writers and artists of his day, and, having thus a connection ready-made, he decided to launch out into picture-dealing. The idea was to eke out his "precarious profits as a man of letters" with a little solid commerce. But he was obviously the worst man in the world for such an enterprise. He was a great deal too honest to cheat his customers and too proud to haggle over prices. Any money he did make he immediately lavished upon his family, which consisted of two boys, William and Francis, the eldest child — a girl — having died a month before William's birth in 1788. The greatest gains he got from the picture-trade were, first: the varied and disillusioning experience which he put into his picaresque novel, *The Memoirs of a Picture,* and secondly: a fund of useful help and training for his artist son.

The Memoirs of a Picture[2] is an odd, rambling piece of work, written in a tone of sustained irony and in a slip-shod kind of mock-heroic English which is vigorous when it forgets to be pretentious. Wilkie, in a pious enthusiasm, has gone so far as to compare the book with Sterne, Smollett and Fielding; but it has not much in common with any of them, beyond diffuseness of plot and liability to stray away into anecdote. Its characters are so vaguely differentiated as to be almost indistinguishable; and the romantic wanderings of the Chevalier Vanderwigtie, the pathetic history of Julia St. Prieux, the coarse amours of Sophia Ogle and the debauches of Mr. Scumble and Mr. Cankergrin are not better, if little worse, than the ordinary eighteenth-century novel of adventure. But where William Collins can stand on his own feet is in his exposure of the tricks of the picture-trade and the universal folly of collectors. Here his special knowledge served him well; and the cheated amateur may note with chagrin that the pits into which he falls to-day were digged for him two hundred years ago, having survived *Quinneys* and every other exposure before and since.

The plot of the book is a malicious travesty of Boccaccio's story of the Three Rings, which Lessing made the text of a sermon, but Collins, of a satire. The "picture" of the title is a

---

[2][Published 1805. Ed.]

masterpiece of "the divine Guido",[3] stolen from a French gallery and fallen into the hands of a Flemish painter, who makes two exact copies of it. In the ensuing adventures of the three pictures, dealers, collectors, professional experts and picture-fakers all in turn are made to display their greed and gullibility. The collectors are fooled by the dealers, the dealers by each other and the experts by everybody. Not only are the copies mistaken for the original; the original itself is solemnly pronounced to be a copy — and a bad one at that: —

> the noble possessor of the illegitimate [should read legitimate— Ed.] offspring of the divine Guido, took an opportunity of gratifying the Chinese connoisseur and his friends with a view of his masterpiece of art; and when their admiration was at the highest, took an opportunity of declaring that this wonderful production was no more than the copy of its divine original, which the uncle of the young artist they saw was in possession of, and who resided in London. Their confusion at this relation could only be equalled by their unparalleled effrontery which succeeded it soon after their recovery. And they declared, that nothing but their respect for so profound a connoisseur could have prevented them from declaring their opinion of its being spurious; though deserving the highest commendation for the faithfulness of its resemblance to the original. "But then," added the chevalier, "your just discrimination could never have overlooked the Flemish gout,[4] evident at the first view of the *tout ensemble*; the eye of the picture is evidently suspicious. — None of the divine expression, none of that downy softness in the cast of the draperies — in short, this group of angels are too gross and fleshy for any but a Flemish master to imagine or embody. — Instead of floating on thin and heavenly aether, you see they are supported by clouds as thick and greasy as pancakes. — Oh, ye divine powers of the immortal Guido! what a treat would the original be to the vision of a kindred professor!"[5]

The experts then hasten to London to purchase the supposed original, which (hoping to beat down the price) they — with unwitting truth — affirm to be a copy. The English dealer, however, is by now in the plot, and sells it to them for a

---

[3]In *Mr. Lepel and the Housekeeper* (Third Epoch) there is a curious little reminiscence of Grandfather Collins' book in the mention of a "Virgin and Child" by Guido, painted on copper, which one of the characters picks up for a song in an out-of-the way shop in Palermo (*Little Novels* [London: Chatto and Windus, 1887], II, 165).

[4]I like to think that English gout is intended, though I fear it is only French *gout* without the circumflex.

[5]*Memoirs of a Picture* (London: H. D. Symonds, 1805), III, Ch. 12 (pp. 166-168).

hundred pounds more than the price he first put upon it when he supposed it to be the original.

All this is extremely good fooling, based as it is upon sound technical knowledge; in addition, the book contains many sly digs at contemporary personages and some very shrewd observations on the art of painting. Old Collins was on the modern side in the artistic quarrel then raging, and his defence[6] of Gainsborough, Reynolds and their school, and of the "national giant" Hogarth, as "natural painters", in contrast to the "old, or black school" is worth reading, particularly in connection with his grandson Wilkie's own art-criticism of a later period.

The only characters in *The Memoirs of a Picture* who are never dishonest or self-deceived in their critical judgments are the painters themselves; for William Collins was the friend of painters, and especially of that unsatisfactory genius, George Morland, whom he loved and befriended to the last. True, his *Life of George Morland,* actually intercalated as Vol. II of the *Memoirs of a Picture* (with which it has nothing at all to do), is rather more candid than charitable; but then, Morland was a man to exasperate even the best of friends. One scene, lingering in the memory of William Collins the younger, and by him handed down to Wilkie, is preserved in the latter's *Memoirs* of his father. It is eloquent of its period, and of the easy-going irregularity of the Collins household. Young William was showing signs of a talent for painting, and his father had promised to obtain for him the aid and advice of Morland.

> For some days the young student had awaited, with mingled anxiety and awe, his promised interview with a man whom he then regarded with all the admiration of the tyro for the professor: but his expectations remained unfulfilled, — the tavern and the sponging-house still held Morland entangled in their toils. At length, one evening, while he was hard at work over a copy, his father entered the room and informed him, with a face of unusual gravity, that Morland was below, but that his introduction to his future master had better be delayed; his impatience, however, to gain a sight of the great man overcame his discretion. He stole softly down stairs, opened the kitchen door, by a sort of instinct, and looked cautiously in. On two old chairs, placed by the

---

[6]*Memoirs of a Picture,* I, Ch. 10 (pp. 138-142).

smouldering fire, sat, or rather lolled, two men, both sunk in the heavy sleep of intoxication. The only light in the room was a small rush candle, which imperfectly displayed the forms of the visitors. One, in spite of the ravages of dissipation, was still a remarkably handsome man, both in face and figure. The other was of immense stature and strength, coarse, and almost brutal in appearance. The first was George Morland; the second, a celebrated prize-fighter of the day, who was the painter's chosen companion at that particular time.

(*Memoirs*, I, 21-22)

Morland might be dissipated as a man and unreliable as a teacher, but he was a genius; old William might be a bad man of business, but he was a remarkable character; the house in Great Portland Street might be besieged by creditors, but it was a place where interesting people congregated: take it all together, young William might have begun his artistic career under worse auspices. Both he and his brother took to drawing at an early age, but William was obviously the destined artist. He had at least so much of genius as consists in an infinite capacity for taking pains. He drew, in season and out of season, everything that he saw, from landscapes to blacking-bottles, till old William began seriously to hope that "he might live long enough to see poor Bill an R. A."

He did not live so long. He saw Bill admitted as an Academy student in 1807 and hung in the same year. In 1808, he saw his first picture sold for four guineas. In the next few years he saw Bill's landscapes and portraits fetching respectable prices, and his own business taking a turn for the better. Then, in 1812, he died, rather unexpectedly, leaving his wife and sons inconsolable and loaded with debt.

Since everything had to be sold to pay the creditors, young William had to buckle to, and support his mother and brother as best he could by his painting. He was not yet twenty-four, and the task looked formidable. Fortunately, he was a youth of almost morbid conscientiousness and industry, and he worked like a galley-slave. His father's connection among patrons of art stood him in good stead. In rapid succession he painted and sold, not only commissioned portraits, but also those *genre* pictures of English rural life of which he made a speciality and which hit the taste of his day so exactly: *The Weary Trumpeter or Juvenile Mischief, The Sale of the Pet Lamb, The Burial-*

place of a Favourite Bird, The Birdcatcher Outwitted, The Kitten Deceived. He kept a diary in which he took severe notice of his own failings and entered sundry reflections upon Art, and the criticisms of his fellow-artists. He observes in himself a tendency to pay too much attention to detail, to the detriment of the general effect. "The whole figure ought to be completely determined on, at the first, or second sitting; after which the parts may be successfully studied" (*Memoirs,* I, 61. His son, Wilkie, was to learn this lesson and profit by it). He harps on the necessity for method, method, more method. "From the great success I have met with, the eagerness I feel to deserve it, and my struggles against sluggishness, I never was more confused in my intellects than now—dreadful want of confidence—my mind must be weeded — method quite necessary — good habits may be gained by watchfulness — bad habits grow of themselves; good ones require cultivation" (*Memoirs,* I, 64).

Not that he was devoid of gaiety and humour. He possessed "a fund of anecdote" which made him welcome in good company, and he could indulge in a quiet practical joke.

> Mr. Leslie, R. A., and an artist named Willis, were guests, one evening, at the painter's house; when Willis left his friends rather abruptly — in spite of their remonstrances — before the usual hour of parting. After he was gone his host sent out for some oysters, and proposed that Willis should be mortified, by being informed of the supper that he had missed through his hasty departure. Accordingly the painter wrote on a large sheet of paper — "After you left us we had oysters;" and sent it, without name or date, or paying postage, (which was then threepence) to Willis. The latter, however, discovered the handwriting; and, to revenge himself, sent back for answer another letter — not paid of course — and only containing the words: — "Had you?" He was nevertheless mistaken, if he imagined that he had beaten his antagonist in brevity; for, the next day, he received, at the price of threepence again, an answer to the interrogatory, "Had you?" in a letter containing the eloquent monosyllable — "Yes!"
> (*Memoirs,* I, 66-67)

He was also deeply appreciative of a good pun, as when his friend James Smith, the "inveterate jester and capital writer," on hearing that Collins was working under the handicap of a severe headache, exclaimed: "Ah ... I see why you have not got on; you are using a new material to-day, — painting in *distemper."* Mirth such as this might well cure any headache; but while Smith had perhaps the advantage in verbal agility, Collins could always call in the resources of his art to the aid of his fancy. He it was who playfully painted on the threshold of his studio the simulacrum of a new pen, and laughed to see his friend stoop down to pick it up — an amiable jest which was to furnish a trait for the portrait of Valentine Blyth.[7]

By 1815, William Collins felt his position to be sufficiently established to justify a move from Great Portland Street to a larger and better house in New Cavendish-street. But the War was only just over, and times were bad, so that in 1816 he found himself "with one sixpence in my pocket, seven hundred pounds in debt, shabby clothes, a fine house, a large stock of my own handyworks, a certainty ... of about a couple of hundreds, and a determination ... of becoming a great painter ... " (*Memoirs,* I, 82). In this determination, he exerted himself harder than ever. Helped by an advance from his father's kind old friend and patron, Sir Thomas Heathcote, he made studies in Norfolk and at Hastings for the seascapes with which he meant to make a fresh appeal to the public. He visited Paris. He fell into difficulties again, and borrowed once more from Sir Thomas. He exhibited whenever he could. He visited Edinburgh and the Lakes, and met Wordsworth and Southey, and became the close friend of Coleridge and of Washington Allston, the American painter. He missed his election to the Academy by a single vote in 1819, but painted on undeterred. He visited Devon, turned the financial corner, and, in 1820, became an Academician at last. To him, this meant much; the magic letters after his name established him socially as well as professionally. To the end of his life, he insisted eagerly upon the title of "Esquire" to which the honour entitled him, and in his will, that title and that honour round off the opening clause which begins so sonorously: "In the Name of God, Amen."

In the year 1822, Collins paid a visit to Edinburgh, in the company of his friend Sir David Wilkie. The object — or at least the ostensible object — of both painters was to see King George

---

[7]In *Hide and Seek* (1854).

IV land at Leith and paint each a picture to commemorate the event. Sir David's picture was duly painted; but Collins, though he saw all the sights and greatly enjoyed the processions and illuminations, had other, private fish to fry. After a brief tour to Blair Adam and Stirling the friends returned to Edinburgh, whence Wilkie went innocently home, leaving Collins behind him.

It will be remembered that Collins had visited Edinburgh before — in 1814, when he possessed more ambition than money. He had then attended a ball, "given by a few artists to their lady friends," where he had met a portionless but attractive young lady, called Harriet Geddes, who was visiting the Edinburgh branch of her family. To his father's son there was something irresistible about a portionless Scottish bride. He was immediately enamoured, though, in his straitened circumstances, too honourable to declare himself. Harriet was one of the five daughters, all beautiful and all artistic of Captain Geddes of Alderbury in Wiltshire. When their father lost his money, the sisters were obliged to earn a living for themselves in London, and here the young couple had found opportunities of meeting from time to time. In 1821 they had at length taken their courage in both hands, and avowed a mutual passion. Harriet was everything that was charming, cultivated and desirable; William was handsome, talented and rising in his profession; and there seemed to be only one obstacle to a happy union. Old Mrs. Collins, retaining dismal memories of hardships undergone when she had been a penniless bride herself, put her foot down. William must wait until his income was more assured — and her opposition was made formidable by "a vexatious Marriage Act, requiring various oaths and attestations from parents and guardians, having lately come into operation in England . . . ."[8]

William heard her prudent counsels, shook his fist at the Marriage Act, and promptly made arrangements to wed his Harriet in Scotland. He wrote to his mother from Edinburgh:

---

[8]The Marriage Act of 18 [22 (3 George IV, c. 75). This act was passed on 22d July 1822; its provisions went into effect on 1st September of that year. The inadequacies of this act were recognized from the beginning, and movements for its amendment or repeal began almost immediately. It was in fact repealed by 4 George IV, c. 17, passed 26th March 1823. Ed.]

> Since I wrote to you last . . . I have been sorely vexed with the toothache and to such a degree at last, that I have discarded my enemy, and am now quite easy. Upon another subject, I am not so gifted with the art of hoping, as at once to expect relief — although the only person on earth who can make me quite happy, is my own dear mother. (*Memoirs*, I, 212-213)

In short, and with all possible duty and respect, he announced his determination to dispense with Mamma's authority as ruthlessly as with the aching grinder. He was married to Harriet Geddes on 16 September 1822 in the English Episcopal Church, in York-place, Edinburgh, by the Rev. Dr. Alison, author of the celebrated work on Taste — and so far as we can tell never had the least reason to regret his reckless act of self-assertion. But it is curious that Wilkie Collins, who later wrote so often and so bitterly in condemnation of the lax marriage laws of Scotland, should have owed his appearance in the world in 1824 to a runaway Scottish marriage.

The first recorded pronouncement upon WILLIAM WILKIE COLLINS is that of his godfather, Sir David Wilkie, who, on being shown the new baby, stared into its eyes and exclaimed with astonishment and delight: "He sees!" The good gentleman, being, as a confirmed bachelor, better acquainted with puppies and kittens than with the human young, was merely noting an interesting physiological fact, but as a piece of prophecy his utterance was not far off the mark. A painter-like faculty of visualization was Wilkie Collins' heritage from two families of artists,[9] and it was with him from the cradle to the grave.

The boy was born on 8th January 1824, according to his own account,[10] at his father's house at 11, New Cavendish-street; according to Thomas Seccombe in the D. N. B. in Tavistock Square. He was at any rate baptised in Saint Marylebone Church, the parish church for New Cavendish Street,[11] and named after his father and godfather. In the following year Mr. Collins — now recognised as a painter of great distinction and busily painting for Academy exhibitions,

---

[9]Harriet Geddes' brother and sisters were all painters. See notes 14 and 16 for this chapter.
[10]Letter to H. J. Nicoll, 28th November 1881.
[11]The parish church for Tavistock Square is Saint Pancras.

for His Majesty the King and for various noble patrons, and filling in his spare time with learning to etch, arranging invitations for R. A. dinners and corresponding with Lord Liverpool on the subject of the recently-founded National Gallery — decided to take up his summer residence at Hendon. Coleridge was then living at Highgate with his friend Gillman, and Collins frequently visited there, and discussed religion with Coleridge and Edward Irving.[12] He returned to 11 New Cavendish-street for the winter, but soon became convinced that it would be better for his work to leave town and live at Hampstead, where he could find, not only peace and fresh air, but also the type of scenery he most wanted to paint. He moved house accordingly and in April 1828 wrote from Hampstead to Sir David Wilkie, then touring in Italy: —

> Your godson grows a strapping fellow, and has a little blue-eyed red-haired bonny bairn, as a brother, about three months old.
> (*Memoirs*, I, 299)

The new baby was Charles Allston Collins, born on January 25th 1828, and named for Washington Allston. His birth, together with the arrival of old Mrs. Collins (now grown very frail) to spend her declining years under her son's roof made a bigger house a necessity. Mr. Collins played for some time with the idea of building one for himself, but, what with legal difficulties about the freehold, and what with the importunity of Sir David Wilkie, who was constantly urging his friend either to join him in Italy or to come and live near him in Kensington, or both, the project fell through. After a trip with the whole family to Boulogne and Ramsgate, Mr. Collins returned to Hampstead and leased a suitable house near the Heath; this, however, was only a temporary abode, and in 1830

---

[12]From Coleridge, Wilkie Collins gained an early insight into the uses and abuses of opium. He told William Winter one day: "I very well remember the poet Coleridge . . . he often came to my father's house, and my father and mother were close friends of his. One day he came there and was in great distress, saying that it was wrong for him to take opium, but that he could not resist the craving for it, although he made every possible effort to do so. His grief was excessive. He even shed tears. At last my mother addressed him, saying: 'Mr. Coleridge, do not cry; if the opium really does you any good, and you *must* have it, why do you not go and get it?' At this the poet ceased to weep, recovered his composure, and, turning to my father, said, with an air of much relief and deep conviction: 'Collins, your wife is an exceedingly sensible woman!' I suppose that he did not long delay to act upon my mother's suggestion. I was a boy at the time, but the incident made a strong impression on my mind, and I could not forget it" (William Winter, *Old Friends* [New York: Moffat, Yard, 1909], pp. 213-214). Coleridge died in 1834, so that Wilkie Collins must have been under ten years of age when he received this vivid impression.

he moved again to Bayswater. But Hampstead and its Heath — then really wild and really romantic — remained deeply imprinted on the heart and mind of "Willy" (as little William Wilkie was called at home). He was to choose it for the great scene of Walter Hartright's first meeting with the Woman in White, and over and over again he came back to it in his later books with a lingering love of its desolate beauty.

In the exercise of his profession, Mr. Collins travelled about England a great deal, both to study the scenery and to execute commissions at the houses of his many patrons, and his life was varied and agreeable. He was no longer the hack worker, called in to restore damaged canvases at a few guineas a time and immortalise the families of country squires at the cheapest rates. He was the Royal Academician, the honored guest of the nobility and gentry,[13] moving with ease and assurance among an aristocracy still powerful and as yet scarcely shaken by the throes of social revolution. It is probably owing to his father's unquestioned social position that young Wilkie grew up to understand, as his greater contemporary Charles Dickens never was able to do, the life and atmosphere of a great English country house and to reproduce it sympathetically, without snobbery or antagonism. Mr. Collins may have had his little weaknesses — he is related to have cut William Blake when he met him in the Strand carrying his own pot of porter — but in his letters there is never the least false note, never the uneasy phantom of the picture-dealer's shop rising shadowy in the background to embarrass him as the phantom of the tailor's establishment embarrassed Meredith. Queer as the old dealer-journalist may have been, he was nothing to be ashamed of, and neither his son nor his grandson ever spoke or wrote of him but with admiring respect and affection.

In spite — or perhaps because — of his frequent absences, the painter was a home-loving man. For his wife he felt a profound and passionate devotion whose sincerity breaks through all the stereotyped phrases of piety in which, after the

---

[13]Including among others Sir Thomas Heathcote, the Duke of Newcastle, the Earl of Lincoln, Sir George Beaumont, Sir Francis Chantrey, Lord de Tabley, the Earl of Liverpool, the Marquis of Camden, Sir Walter Scott, the Earl of Essex, the Duchess of Devonshire, Sir Thomas Lawrence, Sir Robert Peel, the Archbishop of Canterbury, the Marquis of Lansdowne, etc.

manner of his time, he enwraps it. From Patterdale Hall, Penrith, he writes to her in 1832: —

> *The never-to-be-forgotten Sixteenth of September.*
> This is I believe the first return of our wedding day, that we have been separated (in *body*) — in *spirit* we cannot, I pray, be ever asunder. This day, as indeed every day since I have left you, I have drunk your health after dinner, to myself; and am now in my own room, writing another letter to you, on my way towards home.
> (*Memoirs*, II, 17)

And again: —

> about Thursday week, I promise myself the greatest earthly happiness, that of returning to my family — that I loved them greatly I always knew; but how much, never till now.
> (*Memoirs*, II, 18)

He had then been ten years married. Twelve years later, towards the close of his life, he wrote to her in the same sense: —

> My heart troubles me very little, except joyously when I think of home, and of the increasing charms it has for me.
> (*Memoirs*, II, 250)

One would like to know more about Mrs. Collins, who was able to inspire such devoted affection in her husband, her sons and her friends. She seems to have been a woman of great humour and character, as well as of remarkable beauty. She once told Holman Hunt how, when she was a girl, Coleridge had sought her out at an evening party and poured "the highest strains of poetical philosophy" into her ears for twenty minutes. She listened, fascinated by his brilliant blue eyes, but understanding nothing, and wondering what she had done to deserve the honour. To Hunt, looking at a portrait of her painted by her sister Mrs. Carpenter, no explanation was needed.[14] In after days she became, in the words of Leslie Ward, "a quaint old lady who wore her kid boots carefully down on one side and then reversed them and wore them down on the other," and was dreadfully scandalised by the Highland kilt.[15] In the letters of Charles Dickens and in the *Life* of Millais we catch occasional

---

[14] ¶[W. Holman Hunt, *Pre-Raphaelitism and the Pre-Raphaelite Brotherhood,* II (New York: Macmillan, 1906), 187. Ed.] Sarah Margaret Geddes (1793-1872) became a portrait painter in London at the age of 21. Her portrait of Lord Folkestone was hung at the R. A. in 1814. She married (1817) William Carpenter, Keeper of the Prints at the British Museum.

[15] ¶[*Forty Years of 'Spy'* (London: Chatto and Windus, 1915), p. 6. Ed.]

glimpses of her as the kindliest of hostesses to her sons' friends and an entertaining companion, always ready to answer a jest with a jest. With a brother[16] and three sisters who were all artists, she must have been able to give her husband a wealth of intelligent sympathy in his work.

To his sons, William Collins was an affectionate father, edifying and admonitory after the fashionable pattern, but no domestic tyrant, as Wilkie himself at an early age bears testimony:

> Young Wilkie Collins, who was their [the young Linnells'] playmate at Bayswater, was one day in the garden with them, when they happened to draw upon themselves the wrath of their father. Said young Wilkie when the passing storm was over: 'I should not like your father to be mine. Your father is a bull; mine is a cow.'[17]

There seems little reason to doubt the sincerity of this naive and spontaneous tribute. It is true that Mr. Collins had firmly grasped the idea that, on every possible occasion, that occasion must be improved. This was the duty of a parent, and Mr. Collins did not fail in his duty. Since, at this period of his life, his piety took a rather Evangelical turn,[18] the sermonising flavour comes out perhaps a little strongly for our taste in his letters home, where every message points a moral. It is all very well for him to tell his wife how a friend's young son, "a fine little fellow ... about Willie's age, burst out crying during the ride, and after sobbing some time, upon being asked what he was so miserable about, said in the most artless manner, 'Because Mr. Collins is going to leave us!'" A child's appreciation is always flattering, and it was no doubt by a natural

---

[16]Andrew Geddes [1783-1844]. In Horace N. Pym's book, *A Tour round my Book-shelves* (privately printed at Edinburgh by Ballantyne, Hanson, 1891), he mentions four portraits of the Collins family which had passed into his hands after Wilkie Collins' death: "First comes his grandfather, William Collins ... the other little portrait, with its Rembrandt-like colouring, is of the grandmother, who was a Geddes, and both are painted by their son, William Collins .... The next is William Collins himself, painted by his friend Mr. John Linnell ... and lastly, you will see the large picture of the late Wilkie Collins and his brother, Charles Allston Collins, painted when boys by their uncle, Andrew Geddes, A.R.A." (pp. 42-43).

[17]Alfred T. Story, *Life of John Linnell* (London: Richard Bentley, 1892), I, 287.

[18]It is of some interest to note, in passing, a passage from a letter of 1832, written from Kirkby Lonsdale. "To-morrow I hope to hear Mr. Carus Wilson, the rector of this place, to whom I was introduced yesterday. He seems a most amiable man, and bears an excellent character" (*Memoirs*, II, 12). The Brontë children had, of course, long left Cowan Bridge, but *Jane Eyre* had not yet come to shatter Mr. Wilson's peaceful reputation.

association of ideas that Mr. Collins immediately added: "Tell Willie and Charley nothing affords their father more happiness than to hear they are good and attentive to their mother during his absence" (*Memoirs,* II, 14). But it was perhaps a little pointed to write from his next place of call: "Tell the boys that there are two or three really good boys here, and that I trust they have been most excellent children" (*Memoirs,* II, 20). Need he have implied these comparisons? In 1835 he writes again: —

> Tell the dear children that the only way they can serve their parents, is to obey them in all things: let Charley find out the passages in Scripture where this duty is most strongly insisted on, and write them down for me. (*Memoirs,* II, 51)

Charley was seven years old when exhorted to this exercise, and shortly after, he and his eleven-year-old brother were complimented with a letter all to themselves, which begins alarmingly enough, though, like Ophelia's madness, it "turns to favour and to prettiness" further on: —

> Weston House, Sunday morning.
> Dear Willy and Charley, — Your mother's account, in her last letter, of you both, pleased me much. Go on praying to God, through Jesus Christ, to enable you, by his Holy Spirit, to be blessings to your parents; and then you must be happy. Both your letters were well written, and I was delighted to hear you were pleased with the holiday you had on Michaelmas-day. I have made only a few sketches, — one of them, however, will, I think, please you both. It is a drawing of a large gray horse, which was brought to me from the plough. The drawing occupied my time, I dare say, four hours. The horse is evidently of the Flanders breed, and I know Charley always likes to see horses of that class. I think I shall have it framed, and make a present of it to my own Charley. I have a sketch of a water-mill, which I rode many miles yesterday to make, and which, if Willy should take a fancy for, I shall have framed and give to him.
>
> And now, my dear boys, I must leave you, and prepare for going to church, (which we have here in the afternoon,) where I shall pray for my two children and their mother, as well as for all the world besides.
>
> One of the prettiest little robin redbreasts is now singing to me on the balcony of my bedroom, where I am writing. This is as much as to say, — "Come, my master! suppose you go home to your good people at Bayswater, for you know I am not fond of chirping about in this way, until the sharp mornings of October teach me to cultivate my acquaintance with your strapping fellows, who have

so many crumbs that are of no use to you, and which you know we robins consider a great treat!"

A pretty *long* letter, methinks, for two such *short* fellows! However, I never regret any trouble I may have in doing anything for good boys.

From your affectionate father.
WILLIAM COLLINS.
(Memoirs, II, 56-57)

One may take it, I think, that the boys were good boys on the whole, and gave no more trouble than others of their age and sex. One thing and one thing only makes us wonder whether there may not have been some slight spirit of rebellion at home — once a week, let us say. Was that ferocious dislike of evangelical religion which barbs the "Narrative of Miss Clack"[19] prompted by any personal rancour? Is the terrible picture in *Hide and Seek* of a small boy's sufferings under the horrors of a pietistic English Sunday the reflection of Wilkie Collins' own tormented childhood? One hopes not — yet there is reason to fear that it was so. That Papa was solidly Protestant during his early married life is witnessed by a letter dated from Boulogne in 1828, in which he notes that, after attending service at the English church, he and his friends happened to go into a Romish place of worship, where they observed with pity and horror "a figure, full-dressed, nearly as large as life, of the Virgin; which, after being bowed down to and worshipped, was carried in procession on men's shoulders through the church, accompanied by torches, bells, smoke, and other symbols of man's weakness. The expression of devotion," he broadmindedly adds, "on the part of the congregation was deep, and worthy of better teaching" (*Memoirs,* I, 310). Even ten years later, he was guilty of perching himself upon the altar at San Giovanni, to inspect Titian's "Peter Martyr" at close quarters, although he had by this time become a warm supporter of Newman and Pusey and must, one would suppose, have acquired a measure of respect for Catholic symbol (*Memoirs,* II, 145, 250). But in the matter of Sabbath-breaking he was always adamant. His friend Linnell, the artist, who was his near neighbour in Porchester-square, held certain pronounced anti-clerical views and, among other things, had

---

[19] *The Moonstone.*

persuaded himself that the observance of Sunday was contrary to Scripture. He therefore made it a point of conscience to desecrate the Sabbath ostentatiously and on principle. Collins, finding Linnell one fine Sunday afternoon engaged in nailing up peach-trees, was duly horrified. He even went so far as to say (alluding to an entirely unfounded calumny against Linnell which he himself had recklessly helped to spread) that gardening on a Sunday was "ten times worse" than cheating a workman out of his wages, adding that "a man who would break the Sabbath would do any other bad thing" (Story, I, 278). It looks as though we must find a true bill against Mr. Collins in the matter of Sabbatarianism, though we cannot possibly suppose that he actually sat for the portrait of the gloomy and sadistic Mr. Zachary Thorpe.[20] Pompous, opinionated, and something of a prig he undoubtedly was, but he can never have been harsh or violent with the children he loved, and who quite certainly loved him.

We possess a portrait[21] of six-year-old Willy, drawn by his father, which already shows the broad and convex brow overweighting the delicacy of the lower features, and the pouting, sensitive mouth which changed but little in after years. Neither of the boys can ever have been particularly robust; and they probably inherited a certain fragility of constitution from their father's side of the family. William Collins, himself destined to die at the comparatively early age of fifty-nine, had already suffered the loss in 1833, of his beloved brother Frank, who had succumbed to that scourge of the period, typhus, contracted in seaside lodgings at Ramsgate. The death of this brother, who had been his close friend and assistant during the early days of struggle,[22] was a great blow to Mr. Collins, particularly as it was followed, within a few months, by that of their mother.

These bereavements, distressing as they were, had, however, one consequence which was very fortunate for young

---

[20] *Hide and Seek.*
[21] [At the time Sayers wrote this, the portrait was in the possession of Mrs. R. C. Lehmann. At her death, it passed into the hands of the bookseller, Bertram Rota, who sold it to Douglas Ewing of New York City. Ed.]
[22] He was a very skilled picture-restorer, and helped his brother greatly with this remunerative, though uncongenial work.

Wilkie and his brother. They left Mr. Collins free to pursue the plan which Sir David Wilkie had long been urging upon him, namely, to visit Italy and refresh his artistic powers by the study of the Old Masters and the contemplation of Italian scenery. The painter hesitated for some time before making up his mind to this formidable journey, but at length he made the great decision and in September 1836 he packed up bag and baggage and set forth on his travels, taking his whole family with him.

CHAPTER II

At the date of this journey to Italy, Wilkie Collins was between twelve and thirteen years old, and this gives us a date at which we may pause and ask: What about young Wilkie's formal education? Where did he get it, and when? and what was it like?

Where he got it is definitely ascertained — up to a point. He says himself that he was educated in "a private school at Highbury". He does not give exact details, and I have not as yet been able to discover the name of the schoolmaster. *When* he attended this school is less certain, but I am inclined to think that it must have been before, rather than after, the Italian trip. He was a boarder in the school — and this is quite natural, when we consider that his home was at Bayswater, and that, in the days before Underground and the L. G. O. C.,[1] the distance between these two points would have been much too long a journey for a small boy to undertake daily. That he was a small boy at the time is perhaps suggested by the only important reference to his school-days that has come down to us from his own pen: —

> My first efforts at addressing an audience were made before a public of eight boys, in the bedroom at school. The tallest, the strongest, and the oldest boy was placed in authority over us, as captain of the room. He was as fond of hearing stories, in bed, as the oriental despot to whose literary tastes we are indebted for the Arabian Nights. Our tyrant had exhausted the memories, or the imaginations, as the case might be, of the other boys in his room, when I joined the school. On the first night, my capacity for telling stories was tested at a preliminary examination — vanity urged me to do my best — and I paid the penalty. In other words, I was the unhappy boy appointed to amuse the captain from that time forth. It was useless to ask for mercy, and beg leave to go to sleep. "You will go to sleep, Collins, when you have told me a story." In the event of my consenting to keep awake, and to do my best, I was warned beforehand to be amusing if I wished to come out of it with comfort to myself. If I rebelled, the captain possessed an

---

[1][London General Omnibus Company. Ed.]

instrument of correction (an improved cat o' nine tails) invented by himself. He roused his satraps among the other boys, and ordered me to be brought before him in words which I have never forgotten: "Bring Collins out to be thrashed." When I was obstinate I took my thrashing. When my better sense prevailed, I learnt, in the presence of the instrument of correction, to make those calls on my invention which have been pretty often repeated in later years. Like some other despots, the Captain had his intervals of generosity. The most unwholesome things that I have ever eaten were gifts which rewarded me for telling a good story. In after years, I never had the opportunity of reminding him that I had served my apprenticeship to fiction under his superintendence. He went to India with good prospects; and died, poor fellow, a few years only after he had left school.[2]

Now we must reckon the Captain to have been at least seventeen or eighteen at the time of leaving school, since he went abroad "with good prospects" and died "a few years only after"; but it is not necessary to suppose that he was more than fifteen or sixteen at the period of poor Wilkie's sufferings under his rule. Wilkie, on the other hand, must have been either under thirteen (the age at which he left for Italy) or over fifteen (the age at which he returned to England). The one age seems to be rather early for the story-telling; the other, to be rather late for the thrashings. On the whole, I feel it to be slightly less likely that a young man of eighteen or so indulged in the systematic thrashing of even a feeble lad of fifteen, than that a precocious little boy of ten or eleven was a good story-teller. Also, is it very likely that Wilkie received no regular education at all before the age of fifteen? The speculation is a puzzling one, but, take it for all in all, I am disposed, in default of other evidence, to place this harrowing scholastic experience before the Italian tour.[3] In any case, unless Collins began his story-telling at a very early age indeed, the dates show that his school career must have been a short one, and much interrupted.

As to what the education at this school was like, we have two small pieces of direct evidence, for what they are worth. In 1887, Wilkie wrote to a friend:

---

[2] "Reminiscences of a Story-teller," *Universal Review,* May-August 1888, pp. 182-192. The above passage is quoted from the original ms. in the present writer's possession, which contains details omitted from the published version. [See appendix. Ed.]

[3] The *Times* obituary so places it; but the information in these newspaper notices is often inaccurate and cannot be implicitly relied on [(London *Times*, 24th September 1889, p. 5), Ed.]

> That's me, my dear, that's me.
>
> Good God! is "me" grammar? Ought it to be "I"? My poor father paid £90 a year for my education, and I give you my sacred word of honour, I am not sure whether it is "me" or "I."[4]

In those days, £90 a year was a respectable sum, and no doubt Mr. Collins felt that he was doing his best for his eldest boy. If he did not send him to a public school it was either because he did not think the lad's health would stand the strain, or because he and Mrs. Collins could not face the parting. Whether the tuition was worth the sum expended is made a little doubtful — not, indeed, by any hesitation between "I" and "me", which Wilkie Collins could distinguish as well as anybody — but by its general results. Wilkie himself "always expressed the greatest possible contempt for the ordinary methods of English education and, in particular, for the grand old fortifying classical curriculum," says R. Lehmann;[5] and he apparently showed this contempt in a practical manner by forgetting everything he had ever learnt. When called on to assist a school-boy friend to translate an ode of Horace into English verse, he declared that he was "no good at the Latin", but would do his best if supplied with the crib — which he did, turning out a fluent version in heroic couplets.[6] True, he was forty-eight at the time, an age at which many of us find our classical knowledge but a rusty weapon. More serious is the evidence displayed in his whole life and writings that he was not, in the proper sense of the words, a well educated man. His culture was limited; his taste uncertain; his judgment of letters unformed and unreliable; above all, he showed that impatient intolerance of the things he did not like or understand which inevitably betrays a lack of the Humanities. It is, in fact, probable that Highbury — like many other schools — having failed to impart the classics, imparted nothing in particular.

---

[4] Rudolf Chambers Lehmann, *Memories of Half a Century* (London: Smith, Elder, 1908), p. 75.
[5] Page 62.
[6] Page 62. The couplets, (Hor: Lib I. Od:12) which, says R. Lehmann, he dictated "quite as fast as I was able to write them down", are easy and limpid enough in the Pope-and-water manner; the only line which is in any way distinctive or memorable being:

> The might of Claudius grows as forest trees,
> *Which grow, we know not how, by slow degrees*
> *For ever;*

where the monosyllables and the enjambement lift the verse for the moment out of conventionality.

True, Collins has recorded that, in his schooldays, he read Boswell; but the particular passage which evokes this reminiscence is significant. It is that in which Johnson deprecates rigid adherence to a set plan of study and concludes that "a man ought to read just as inclination leads him; for what he reads as a task will do him little good." Wilkie's comment is: "What a consolation [those admirable words] were to me when I could not learn my lesson!"[7]

Indeed, one suspects that Dr. Johnson's advice was taken fairly often and interpreted pretty liberally. According to his own account, Wilkie was no more industrious at his task than many another famous man.

> When I was at school, — perpetually getting punished as "a bad boy," — the master used to turn me to good moral account, as a means of making his model scholars ashamed of their occasional lapses into misconduct: "If it had been Collins I should not have felt shocked and surprised. Nobody *expects* anything of *him*. But You!!" — etc., etc.[8]

Possibly our young hero's mind was not on his work, for at the age of twelve years he was in the throes of his first love-affair. The object of his flame was, naturally, a married woman at least three times his own age, and he suffered horribly from jealousy of the lady's husband. Whenever that excellent and inoffensive person hove in sight, Wilkie would rush madly away, unable to abide the detested presence.[9]

Upon this idyllic and, in the nature of things, hopeless passion, the Italian journey ruthlessly intruded. New interests and new images banished the dream of love; a wide horizon

---

[7]"Books Necessary for a Liberal Education," *Pall Mall Gazette,* 11th February 1886, p. 2.
[8]Letter to William Winter, 3d September 1881, quoted in *Old Friends* (New York: Moffat, Yard, 1909), p. 218. See also *The Lazy Tour of Two Idle Prentices,* [where Idle, that is, Collins, reflects that all the great disasters of his life have occurred as a result of his being lured into an unwonted activity. At school, the evil example of an industrious companion led him to compete successfully for a school prize. As a result, he lost face with his fellow students, good and bad, and with his teachers: "Never again did he hear the head-master say reproachfully to an industrious boy who had committed a fault, 'I might have expected this in Thomas Idle, but it is inexcusable, sir, in you, who know better'" (London: Chapman and Hall, 1890), pp. 56-57. Ed.]
[9]Wolzogen: p. 11 [This paragraph re-states a sentence in Ernst von Wolzogen's *Wilkie Collins: Ein biographisch-kritischer Versuch* (Leipzig: von Unflad, 1885), p. 11: "Im Alter von zwölf Jahren nämlich entbrannte sein Herz für eine mindestens dreimal so alte verheirathete Frau und seine Eifersucht auf deren vortrefflichen Gemahl war so heftig, dass er seine Nähe nicht ertragen konnte, sondern davonlief, wenn er ihn kommen sah". Ed.]

opened up before the eyes of the young artist and story-teller; his receptive mind was subjected to the stamp of new and powerful impressions. Mr. Collins, whether or not he was wise in his choice of a school, at least did brilliantly well for his eldest son in thus taking him abroad and showing him the ancient and modern worlds. In Rome herself, Wilkie discovered all the glamour which had escaped him in the pages of Virgil; and whatever he learned of ancient history and civilization seems to have had its root in this early travel experience, being fed and watered, of course, by the novels of Bulwer-Lytton. It was a piece of luck such as falls to the lot of very few boys — the gift of these two splendid years, spent travelling about Italy, not as a tourist, but as the companion of a highly intelligent artist. Charley, at nine, was too young to profit very much, but Wilkie was just old enough to receive and retain what he saw and heard in his rapidly-expanding mind.

The family party left Dover on 19th September, crossing by way of Boulogne, and taking the diligence to Amiens and thence to Paris. Ten days of bad weather were spent in seeing the Louvre and the sights, and they passed on to Auxerre. Here Mr. Collins lost patience with the diligence — he was always very much the Englishman abroad — and they went on by post to Châlon, thence by boat to Lyon and Arles, and so to Marseilles, passing through Martigues — "built upon piles, surrounded by water like a miniature Venice, inhabited by a race of people who seemed half-smugglers and half-fishermen, and furnished with one small inn, the master of which, never having seen an Englishman before, sat down to dinner with his customers, and kept his cap on with edifying independence."[10] It is good to learn, at twelve years old, that foreigners can show independence, and that all towns are not built like London. From Marseilles (pronounced dirty and dull) they journeyed across the passes to Toulon — by moonlight through Luc to Cannes — and thence, between the Alps and the Mediterranean, to Nice, "the gates of Italy". There is possibly something to be said for traveling in this manner, rather than by wagon-lit-de-luxe; however, the charm of nineteenth-century travel was succeeded by the draw-backs of nineteenth-century

---

[10] *Memoirs of the Life of William Collins, Esq., R. A.* (London: Longman, Brown, Green, and Longmans, 1848), II, 76.

drainage: the cholera was raging in Italy, and the journey had to be delayed for six weeks, during which Mr. Collins sketched assiduously, and his biographer notes with surprise "the changeable climate of the place . . . it was no uncommon sight at Nice, to perceive the countrywomen making hay on one day in November, and carrying their wares to market ankle-deep in rain, water, and mud the next. It was no uncommon occurrence to shade yourself one morning with an umbrella from the sun, and to fortify yourself the next with a great coat against the cold" (*Memoirs*, II, 84). To be sure, this is no uncommmon occurrence in England either, but the English suppose themselves to have a copyright in the weather; Wilkie's insular illusions were thus early dispelled. On December 14th, they set forth again, taking the Cornice road to Genoa, with Mr. Collins "nearly driven mad" by the beauty of everything he saw, hanging out of the carriage-window and trying to sketch the scenery as they rolled past it. Four days at Genoa — a moonlight voyage to Leghorn and thence by road to Pisa — then, dazzled with the glories of Veronese and Vandyke, "gorgeous architecture" and the frescoes of the Campo Santo, to Florence, which they reached on December 24th to find the city in the grip of an old-fashioned English Christmas, with snow knee-deep in the streets, immense icicles hanging from the water-spouts and a piercing wind.

More picture galleries, chapels, churches, bronzes, bridges, statues — as many as could be crammed into a week's stay; and then, a fearful journey, occupying six days, "by way of Sienna, over the frost-bound Apennines at the rate of a road-wagon", to Rome, the shrine of the painter's pilgrimage. Here Mr. Collins, regretfully abandoning his first project of hiring the house once occupied by Claude and painting in his studio — "the rooms were found to be so dirty, and the character of the landlord so bad" — secured comfortable lodgings and at once sat down to unburden himself to Sir David Wilkie of his first impressions of Raphael and Michael Angelo. The Vatican frescoes surpassed all that he had ever conceived of those truly inspired men. He could scarcely write until he had come to his senses; — nevertheless, he kept his head about the "Transfiguration", voting it "hard and mechanical, and only saved by the wonderful expression in some of the faces and figures . . . ."

What Wilkie thought of these masterpieces at the time is not recorded; in later years he was considerably more critical than Papa — but then, he was to complete his artistic education among the Pre-Raphaelites. In the meantime, he made himself acquainted with the streets and monuments of the city, and stored up mental pictures for future use.

The next place on the Collins itinerary was Naples — and, although the cholera was reported to have broken out there, Mr. Collins left Rome after Easter and spent three weeks in that maritime lotos-land. By this time, however, the ominous appearance in the streets of strange yellow sedan-chairs, carrying the cholera victims to hospital, had begun to impress even him with the necessity of taking the pestilence seriously. He departed hastily to Sorrento, only just escaping being shut up in quarantine within the plague-stricken city. Sorrento provided plenty of subjects for landscapes and sea-scapes; while the "old lay-brother at the convent, who, provided he were well supplied with snuff, was perfectly willing to figure on the artist's canvas whenever he chose to paint him", probably sat, unconsciously, for his word-portrait at the same time, being later immortalised in the tale of *Mad Monkton* (*Memoirs*, II, 109).

It was at Sorrento that poor Mr. Collins, who had all the unimaginative virtues of a Briton, contrived to do a very foolish thing, which might well have slain him on the spot, and did actually prove the death of him in the long run.

> Such of his friends at Sorrento as were residents there, constantly entreated him, as they saw him set forth, day after day, on his sketching excursions, not to risk exposure to the noon-tide heat, but to take the usual "siesta" enjoyed by the Italians during the middle of the day. Remonstrances of this kind were, however, in vain; he met all objections, by declaring that he had not come all the way to Italy to go to sleep in the daylight — that he could not remain within the house, even for an hour, while there was anything left to sketch without — and that he trusted to his temperate habits and good constitution, to enable him to follow his occupations, in his own way, with impunity. (*Memoirs*, II, 111)

Alas! even temperance and the British constitution did not avail against the laws of Nature. Shivering, sickness and pains in the head and limbs seized on the intrepid man at the end of a long July day spent toiling under the unforgiving sun. The attack settled down into what appears to have been a kind of rheumatic fever, fastening itself upon the right hand, arm and shoulder and the left leg, and next, upon the eyes, and ending in complete prostration. He remained a helpless invalid until October, when the doctor packed him off to the sulphur-baths at Ischia. These effected a partial cure, and after a month's treatment, he was able to go back to Naples — now cholera-free — and to resume his work and travels. He was, however, never quite the same man again. In view of the fact that Wilkie, in his turn, was to suffer tortures for the greater part of his life from rheumatism and gout in his eyes, it seems likely that there was a hereditary pre-disposition to this kind of trouble. Or possibly the Italian indiscretions sowed the seeds of the disease in the son as well as in the father, since William Collins no doubt imposed his own Spartan habits on the whole family.

During the rest of their stay in Italy, the Collinses saw many beautiful and many strange, surprising things. There was a monk, vowed to poverty, publicly tried at Naples for murdering a woman for her money; there was the "demoralizing business" of the draw for the State Lottery "sanctioned by the presence of many judges, (some in cocked hats), and even by what is termed the Church"; there was a queer incident of a priest who had an intrigue with a gentleman's wife, and, on its being discovered, hired a barber to murder the gentleman for a hundred ducats — which he did! There was the cathedral at Scala, where "a miserable, dirty old woman showed us a nasty mitre, worked all over with pearls and precious stones"; there were crags and castles, valleys and fishing-towns, goat-herds and mule-drivers, producing altogether the most enchanting pictures on the road between Amalfi and Vietri; there were several letters lost in the post — very mortifying; there was Vesuvius, "whose original and beautiful shape was sacrificed to fulfil an act of Divine justice" by overwhelming the profligate city of Pompeii; there was a grotto; and there was poor Charley, who had a fall and seriously damaged himself. All these things brought them to the spring of 1838, when they began the long trek homeward going from Rome, by way of Florence, Bologna, Parma, Verona, and Padua, to Venice, where they made a month's stay and found everything as picturesque and beautiful as could be expected.

This was the end of the tour. They returned through Innspruck, Salzburg, Munich (where Mr. Collins saw the productions of the modern German school, and was not impressed), Mannheim and Heidelberg. Thence they embarked upon the Rhine, whose scenery was voted much inferior to the beauties they had previously seen, and so, "after a passing look at Mayence and Cologne", to Rotterdam. Finally, they reached home on 15th August 1838, having been abroad almost two years, and missed, incidentally, the Queen's Coronation and the greater part of the *Pickwick Papers*.[11]

The years 1839 and 1840 were remarkable for no particular incident, except for successive house-removals, first to Avenue Road, Regent's Park, secondly, to 85, Oxford-terrace. Mr. Collins was busy making pictures from his wealth of Italian material, while Wilkie was, perhaps, completing his interrupted education, either in England or abroad. No very clear light is thrown on these two years by any biographical notice. The *Daily Telegraph* thinks that "his father was somewhat at a loss with regard to his future prospects";[12] the *Daily News,* on I know not what grounds, hazards that "he seems to have been intended for the Church"; most writers content themselves with saying, vaguely, that "on his return from Italy", or "after a brief schooling in England and Italy", he was articled (and here they are all agreed) to the firm of Antrobus and Company, tea-traders in the City. Even so, a slight difficulty arises about the date. The D. N. B. gives it definitely as 1841. The objection to this is that early in June 1842 we find him cheerfully setting out with his father for a trip to the Shetlands, lasting about a month. Either newly-articled clerks in those days received better holidays than they do to-day, or Mr. Antrobus was particularly generous in this instance, or the date is wrong. In view of the fact that William Collins had exhibited a portrait of Mr. Antrobus and his children in the Academy of 1842, I am inclined to think that the business career of young Wilkie may

---

[11] Publication in weekly parts began Jan: 1836. [Actually, publication in monthly numbers ran from 31st March 1836 to 30th October 1837. Ed.]

[12] [The obit. in the *Daily Telegraph,* 24th September 1889, which Miss Sayers cites, does not contain these words. They appear in the *Illustrated London News's* obit., 28th September 1889. Ed.]

have been fixed up during the sittings and begun in 1842 and that the Shetland expedition was thus meant to be his last free fling, before settling down to the drudgery of the office.

This trip to the Shetlands was undertaken in order that Mr. Collins might make a set of illustrations for the "Abbotsford" edition of *The Pirate*. Although the rheumatic fever contracted in Italy had now resulted in a definitely diseased condition of the heart, the painter pluckily undertook a journey far rougher and more laborious than it would be to-day, and thoroughly enjoyed the wild scenery and quaint manners and customs of the islands. Wilkie, in the *Memoirs,* gives a lively description of the party, "Mr. Collins, with one knee on the ground, steadying himself against the wind; his companion holding a tattered umbrella over him, to keep the rain off his sketch-book; the guide standing by, staring at his occupation in astonishment; and the ponies browsing near their riders, on the faded grass, with mane and tail ever and anon floating out like streamers on the gusty breezes that swept past them" (II, 223).

The interlude was soon over, and young Wilkie found himself tied down to a desk in a City office, playing the idle apprentice and dreaming, among the ledgers and the bills of lading, of the moon-lit glamour of the Colosseum. He discovered in himself no liking for commerce at all, and was, indeed, secretly engaged upon something far more interesting and exciting. He was writing a romance, which dealt in the best Bulwer-Lytton manner, with the fall of Rome and the victories of Alaric the Goth. He wrote part of it and then, with hope and fear, submitted the manuscript to his father. If only Papa thought well of it perhaps he would allow his son to leave the obnoxious office and devote himself to art or literature — at least to something less dreary than the tea-trade.

To William Collins' lasting honour be it recorded that he at once took a most enlightened view of the matter. He was immensely pleased. Possibly like Mr. Thorpe in *Hide and Seek,* he began by urging the usual considerations about the benefits of a settled career and the propriety of remaining in the state of life to which one's parents had called one. But before long he recognised that Wilkie really had a call to something in the literary and artistic way; he promptly released him from

Mincing Lane and, having too much sense to keep the youngster hanging about at home, started him off again in a new profession which would occupy his mind and yet give him leisure and opportunity to write books. He entered him at Lincoln's Inn in May 1846 and set him to study for the Bar.

Whether Wilkie himself ever seriously expected or intended to make the law his life-work is rather doubtful; he says himself that his law-studies lasted only a few months. But he must have done rather more at Lincoln's Inn than eat his dinners, for he certainly obtained a legal grounding which came in very useful in his later work. One cannot mistake the distinctively legal attitude of mind which permeates all his work. It has been objected that all Collins' characters argue like lawyers in a manner more characteristic of the author than of themselves,[13] and there is truth in the objection; but it is exactly this fact which gives to his "sensation" novels their curiously satisfying intellectual quality. His training, in the law, moreover, supplied him with much of the actual plot material and machinery for his future books, particularly in connection with the obscurities of the marriage-laws of the three kingdoms and the laws affecting property and inheritance.

At the time, however, he had not turned his mind in the direction of the sensation novel. The first published work of his that is known to exist is a short article called *The Last Stage-Coachman,* written at the age of nineteen and printed in Douglas Jerrold's *Illuminated Magazine* for 1843. It is a delicate and pleasing little study, lamenting the disappearance of the old stage-coaches before the invasion of the railway, and is written with more simplicity than one expects from a young man. The touches of cockney humour and pathos are obviously modelled on Dickens, as at that date they were bound to be; some vivid touches of description already betray the eye and hand of the artist. Probably there are many other fugitive

---

[13]Dickens wrote to Collins, about *The Woman in White:* "I seem to have noticed, here and there, that the great pains you take express themselves a trifle too much . . . . I find it difficult to take out an instance of this. It rather belongs to your habit of thought and manner of going about the work. Perhaps I express my meaning best when I say that the three people who write the narratives in these proofs have a DISSECTIVE property in common, which is essentially not theirs but yours; and that my own effort would be to strike more of what is got *that way* out of them by collision with one another, and by the working of the story" (*Letters of Charles Dickens* [London: Macmillan, 1893], p. 492).

pieces of the same kind hidden in the columns of the magazines of the day. The Roman novel appears to have been laid aside for the time being, for it is recorded that Wilkie's first completed work was a romance dealing with life among the islanders of Tahiti before their discovery by civilised man. It is perhaps not surprising that this work was "declined in turns by every publisher in London". The subject, thought no doubt "interesting as an indication of that bent towards the wild and remote which is characteristic of so many of his later inventions",[14] can hardly have been suited to his talent, and the total disappearance of the ms. is probably no great loss to the world. Undeterred by failure, he took up *Antonina or the Fall of Rome* again,[15] and wrote the first volume and half of the second in his evenings, when his law-studies were done, seated in his own corner of the studio where his father, now a sick and prematurely failing man, toiled undauntedly upon his canvases. In 1843 the family had again moved house—this time into Devonport Street where, for the first time in his laborious life, William Collins found himself in possession of a really commodious "painting-room", properly fitted up for his occupation, —

> with more of his sketches, his designs, his relics of Art, about him, than he had ever been able to range in any former studio — with his painting-table, that had belonged to Gainsborough, with his little model of an old woman, dressed by the same great painter's hand; with the favorite palettes of Lawrence and Wilkie,[16] hung up before him; with all the other curiosities, experiments, and studies in Art, that he had collected, now for the first time conveniently disposed around him. (*Memoirs*, II, 244)

The bond of cheerful affection between the father and his sons had never been closer than in these last years of the painter's life. Both boys gave good promise of fulfilling those hopes of a useful and distinguished career which were the subject of Mr. Collins' fervent and earnest prayer. "Willy" had his writing and his law studies, while Charley already displayed a talent for painting which encouraged the belief that he was destined to follow in his father's footsteps. "I most fully and sincerely believe", wrote Mr. Collins in his diary,

---

[14]*Daily News*, 24th September 1889.
[15]The existing ms. records that this draft was begun on April 23rd 1846.
[16]Sir David Wilkie had died in 1841.

"that, if this boy [Charley] does justice to the genius with which he is endowed, and with the blessing of health — which most fervently I pray the Giver of all good to bestow upon him — he will, with his tact and taste, produce most satisfactory and popular works" (*Memoirs,* II, 287). Mr. Collins certainly did not intend anticlimax when uttering this fervent aspiration; his own work had always been eminently satisfactory and popular and he could desire nothing better for Charley, of whom he always seems to speak with especial tenderness. Probably of the two boys Charley was the more in tune with his father's mind: he shared to the full the Tractarian enthusiasm which apparently left Wilkie unmoved, and he was, throughout his brief life, a person of singular sensitiveness and charm.

In these happy circumstances, fame achieved, affluence assured, and surrounded by a united and affectionate family, the painter might well have hoped to enjoy a halcyon summer of existence. In spite of increasing ill-health, he worked at his canvases "with all the buoyant delight, and more than the ardent ambition of his younger days" (*Memoirs,* II, 244). But the mischief done in Italy could not be undone. A continual, wearing cough made its appearance, accompanied by alarming shortness of breath and cardiac symptoms. Change of air was tried in vain. His nights were made torment by insomnia and his days, by dyspepsia. Constant colds and sore throats harassed and weakened him. Sir Benjamin Brodie, seeing him thus devitalised, suggested that he should be cupped and bled, but finding the patient's good sense opposed to this lowering treatment, took refuge in advising quiet of mind and body. By 1846, Mr. Collins seemed only able to drag out existence from one moment to the other; his heart, "appearing not to beat, but to heave with a rushing, irregular, watery sound", his breathing "oppressed, as in the last stages of asthma", his cough assailing him "with paroxysms so violent ... as to create apprehension that he might rupture a blood-vessel ... " (*Memoirs,* II, 281). He could not lie down; he could not sleep; he complained that his nerves, especially of the stomach, seemed to be "alive"; they drenched him with drugs, which only made him worse; dropsy set in and crippled him hand and foot. With dogged and indomitable energy he still struggled to paint — the brush dropping from his hand for sheer weakness, or laid aside while he gasped and struggled for breath. In this terrible last year he yet contrived to complete four important pictures. The doctors declared that he could not see the year out, but "the January of 1847 approached, and he still existed" — still in a few faint and almost unintelligible lines, would try to put down on paper some little arrangement of form and colour.

On the evening of the 16th February, Wilkie, toiling at his Roman novel, his short-sighted eyes bent close to the line of minute and cobweb-fine handwriting, laid down his pen in the middle of a paragraph, to stand by his father's death-bed. The unfinished page still stands in the manuscript — left, by a restrained and touching gesture of filial piety, blank, except for a commemorative note: —

> Thus far I have written during my father's lifetime — This portion of Chapter 3rd was composed on the last evening when he was alive — I now — in returning to my work — leave this page and continue on the next — *"In Caelo Quies"* — W. W. C. July 25th 1847.

Chapter III

William Collins, like his father before him, died leaving a widow and two sons; but, unlike his father, he left his family in easy circumstances: his devoted industry had not been in vain. Wilkie was able to continue his studies for the bar and his literary pursuits, and it was natural that he should temporarily lay aside Polynesian and early-Christian romances and turn his attention to preparing a memorial of his father.[1] He set about this work of piety at once and, for an entirely inexperienced biographer of twenty-three, he did very well with it. His orderly habit of mind stood him in good stead, and he grasped the basic principle of biographical success, namely, to give the facts without unnecessary comment and to allow the subject to speak for himself as far as possible in diaries and letters. The two volumes of the *Memoirs*[2] are written in a pleasant, unpretentious style; they are perhaps a little stiff and formal in places, a little diffuse here and there, but they present a clear and unmistakable portrait of the man and have the by no means common merit of describing a perfectly virtuous character without alienating the reader's sympathy. The *Memoirs* are, as was to be expected, wholly laudatory: there is no attempt at impartial criticism either of the painter's character or of his art; we hear nothing about the Sabbatarian dispute with Linnell, about the incident of his meeting Blake in the Strand carrying a pot of porter, and cutting him; but touches of genuine humour are by no means lacking, and owing to the perfect simplicity of its treatment, the book is neither pompous nor dull. We might to-day be willing to spare some of the lengthy descriptions of Academy pictures, but in the life of a

---

[1] It had been already suggested, in Mr. Collins' lifetime, that Wilkie should undertake this task. On January 1st 1844, Mr. Collins had written in his journal: "As I think it quite possible that my dear son, William Wilkie Collins, may be tempted, should it please God to spare his life beyond that of his father, to furnish the world with a memoir of my life, I purpose occasionally noting down some circumstances as leading points, which may be useful" (*Memoirs,* II, 247). This project was, however, never carried out.
[2] *Memoirs of the Life of William Collins, Esq., R. A. with selections from his Journals and correspondence.* By his son, W. Wilkie Collins. London: Longman, Brown, Green, and Longmans. MDCCCXLVIII (2 vols.).

distinguished painter such passages are proper enough; and when Wilkie turns from cataloguing canvasses to describing scenes from nature he can show a pretty skill in word-painting. Several extracts from the *Memoirs* have already been given in the course of the last two chapters; it will be enough to give one more passage, taken from the account of the tour in the Shetlands: —

> The day after the expedition to Sumburgh Head, (which ended on the part of the Shetland ponies in one of them running away, after a forty miles' journey, when he found himself near his stable!) a large fleet of Dutch herring-boats anchored in Lerwick Harbour, and considerably enlivened its generally vacant appearance. The sight of these vessels recalled to my father his old favourite studies among the fishermen of the English shores, and animated him with the desire of examining them, to discover any elements of the picturesque among their crews, and any varieties between the rig of a Dutch and an English fishing-boat. Accordingly he and his companion mounted the side of the outermost of the clumsy little vessels, (which were all regularly ranged side by side, like volumes of Hume and Smollett on a school-room bookshelf,) but without finding any one on board. A second, third, and fourth proved equally solitary; but in the fifth and largest of the small squadron, they found signs of life. Two portly Dutchmen, utterly drunk and perfectly good-humoured, received them on deck, and led them, — allowing the painter little time to make any pictorial observations of their vessel or themselves, — down a ladder into a dark wooden pit, smelling strongly of stale herrings, called the cabin; in which sat the skipper, a man of vast breeches and cloudy physiognomy. After a few words in Dutch between him and his crew, — neither of the three speaking a word of English, — the captain pulled from a shelf a bottle of "schnapps," three glasses, and a map of Europe. Having poured out the spirit, he spread forth the map on a locker, slowly placed his thumb on that part of it occupied by England, nodded his head solemnly at his guests, and drank off his dram in utter silence. He then pushed the map to the painter and his companion, who, finding it necessary to act their parts in this pantomime of international amity, put their thumbs on Holland, nodded their heads, and emptied their glasses in humble imitation of their host. Ludicrous as this part of the interview was, the scene became doubly comical when the painter, first making a series of elaborate signs, and then, in despair, speaking English with as strong a Dutch accent as he could assume impromptu, endeavoured to make the captain understand that he wanted to sketch from his vessel and his crew. All was in vain; this worthy man had but one idea in his head, and that was Bacchanalian. He nodded again, and prepared to fill the glasses once more: a course of

proceeding which immediately drove Mr. Collins on deck. Here he had no better success with the crew. A gift of money produced a present of a bagfull of herrings; and more of the Anglo-Dutch, a hail for a shore boat. Finding the sketch-book an inscrutable mystery to the Hollanders, and fearing a further invasion of "schnapps" and herrings, the painter (who was by this time inarticulate with laughter) joined his companion in the boat that had now come alongside, and left the Dutchmen to continue their potations in peace. (*Memoirs,* II, 220-222)

The thing has been seen; the figures live and move; Mr. Collins, talking English with a foreign accent after the manner of Mrs. Plornish,³ is presented without comment, amiably and indomitably British. There is nothing in the *Memoirs* to foreshadow Wilkie Collins, the master of constructional form, but there are pages from which the wise might have prophesied the brilliant landscapes of *No Name* and *Armadale* and the solid portrait-painting of *The Moonstone* and *Poor Miss Finch*.

The book, published by subscription, was widely read — owing chiefly, no doubt, to the great popularity of its subject — and it must have served to establish young Collins in the eyes of the publishing world as a "jeune homme sérieux," whose manuscripts could be treated with respect. His next manuscript was such as to justify this view. It would, as one critic⁴ has remarked, "have satisfied the Ministerial dispenser of literary pensions . . . ." It was, in fact, *Antonina or the Fall of Rome,*⁵ duly completed and partly re-written and furnished with a prefatory certificate of historical accuracy.⁶ It was accepted by Richard Bentley, and published in 1850, in three handsome volumes in cream embossed cloth with tooled gilt spine.

It was in this year⁷ that Millais painted the very fine

---

³[[In *Little Dorrit* (Bk. I, Ch. xxv). Ed.]]

⁴*Daily Telegraph,* 24th September 1889, p. 3

⁵*Antonina; or, The Fall of Rome.* A Romance of the Fifth Century. By W. Wilkie Collins, author of the Life of William Collins, R. A. London: Richard Bentley, MDCCCL. 3 vols.

⁶"Whenever it has been thought probable that some desire might be felt to test the historical accuracy of particular passages, the proper notes have been inserted . . . the reader is referred to the Appendix at the end of each Volume . . . . the Author has taken care to refer, on all possible occasions, to the 'Decline and Fall of the Roman Empire' . . . " (Preface, pp. viii-ix).

⁷[[That is, 1850. Miss Sayers followed here the dating of the National Portrait Gallery, noting that it is wrongly dated in John G. Millais' *Life and Letters of Sir John Everett Millais,* where it is dated "*Circ* 1855" 2d edn. (London: Methuen, 1900), I, 279, and finding some support for the Gallery dating in W. Holman Hunt's statement that it was done while Wilkie was writing *Mr. Wray's Cash-Box (Pre-Raphaelitism and the Pre-*

portrait of Wilkie Collins which is now in the National Portrait Gallery. We recognize it unmistakably as the likeness of a young man engaged in an important work involving much historical research. It strikingly shows the massive forehead with the noticeable bulge on the right-hand side concerning which Collins was wont to complain that "Nature in his case had been a 'bad artist' who had depicted his forehead 'all out of drawing'",[8] while Holman Hunt considered that it was no disfigurement but perhaps even "gave a stronger impression of intellectual power" (*Pre-Raphaelitism,* I, 304). The eyes, already bespectacled, but not yet clouded with gout and opium, are large and grey, with long lashes; the mouth still keeps its childish pout; the chubby chin and small fleshy hands give promise of plumpness in later years. Two handsome rings, an impressive shirt-stud, a massive watch-chain and a certain luxuriance of collar and tie suggest that our author thought none too badly of his own appearance, despite his short stature (five feet six inches) and rather top-heavy figure. The expression is one of extreme, almost owl-like solemnity, but, actually young Collins was a lively lad enough, brimming over with fun and ready to take a hand in anything. It was with enormous delight that in 1848 he had engineering the elopement of his friend E. M. Ward with a young lady of fifteen, whose parents, not unnaturally, objected to such an early marriage. "Wilkie Collins", says Mrs. Ward, "played an important part in our plot; he impressed great caution and secrecy, as he planned out the whole affair with zest and enjoyment." Many was the secret marriage which he was thereafter to plot on paper with the same rich gusto for cunning contrivance and romantic atmosphere: no wonder Mrs. Ward observed that he was "in his element. The spice of romance and mischief appealed to him; he gave me away to the best of men, with a hearty good will. . . . My sister-in-law and Wilkie Collins saw us into a cab for her home, and off we started. The cab was held up for some time by a crowd surrounding a belated May-Day 'Jack-in-the-Green,' a man dressed in fantastic attire with green boughs and leaves, walking on stilts. He looked into our window and grinned with delight. . . ." After which Wilkie and

---

Raphaelite Brotherhood, II [New York: Macmillan, 1906], 185). She concluded that it "therefore *must* be earlier than 1852." Ed.]
[8][*Daily Telegraph,* 24th September 1889, p. 3. Ed.]

Portrait of Wilkie Collins (1850) by John Everett Millais.
Courtesy of National Portrait Gallery.

his brother solemnly dined in Grove End Road with the bride and her blandly unconscious parents, and three months later, when Henrietta Ward ran away to join her husband it was Wilkie Collins "who played the part of fairy godmother" to them and found them rooms for their honeymoon. Pretty well, indeed, for a young man of twenty-four. No wonder that, when he came to write *Armadale,* Wilkie Collins found himself remarkably well up in the law relating to the marriage of minors. However, the bride's parents had apparently no objections to the match except their daughter's youth; they accepted the *fait accompli,* and no worse punishment happened to Wilkie Collins than to be made godfather to the first child of the marriage and to become slightly hilarious at the christening.[9]

There was, however, nothing in the least hilarious about the new novel. Compared with the *Memoirs* which preceded it, *Antonina* shows at first sight, a falling-off in almost every respect. It contrives to be at one and the same time impossibly melodramatic and impossibly dull; the language is pompous and old-fashioned; the style derivative; the characters stereotyped; from first to last no gleam of humour enlivens its closely-printed and rhetorical pages. It is the eighteenth century at its antithetical worst: —

> Never was popularity more unalloyed than Vetranio's. Gifted with a disposition, the pliability of which adapted itself to all emergencies, his generosity disarmed enemies, while his affability made friends. Munificent without assumption, successful without pride, he obliged with grace, and shone with safety. People enjoyed his hospitality, for they knew that it was disinterested; and admired his acquirements, for they felt that they were unobtrusive.
> (I, 71-72)

> Darkness had no obscurity that forced him to repose, and lassitude no eloquence that lured him to delay. (II, 9)

It is Bulwer at his most turgid: —

> The next moment — when the guests started up to question or deride him — he turned slowly and faced them. Desperate and

---

[9][Miss Sayers cites as her source for this information Stewart M. Ellis' *Wilkie Collins, Le Fanu, and Others* (London: Constable, 1931), pp. 10-12. Direct quotations the editor has checked against the original passages in Henrietta (that is, Mrs. E. M.) Ward's *Memories of Ninety Years,* 2d edn. (New York: Henry Holt, n. d.), pp. 38-40, 52. Details about Wilkie's behavior at the christening are from Ellis, not Mrs. Ward.]

drunken as they were, his look awed them into utter silence. His face was deathlike in hue, as the face of the corpse above him — thick drops of perspiration trickled down it like rain — his dry, glaring eyes, wandered fiercely over the startled countenances before him; and as he extended towards them his clenched hands, he muttered in a deep gasping whisper: — "Who has done this? MY MOTHER! MY MOTHER!" (III, 106-107)

It is nineteenth-century cardboard Gothic at its most sentimental: —

> As the last sounds of her voice and her lute died softly away upon the still night air, an indescribable elevation appeared in the girl's countenance. She looked up rapturously into the far, star-bright sky; her lip quivered; her dark eyes filled with tears, and her bosom heaved with the excess of the emotions that the music and the scene inspired. Then she gazed slowly around her, dwelling tenderly upon the fragrant flower-beds that were the work of her own hands, and looking forth with an expression half reverential, half ecstatic, over the long, smooth, shining plains, and the still, glorious mountains, that had so long been the inspiration of her most cherished thoughts, and that now glowed before her eyes, soft and beautiful as her dreams on her virgin couch. Etc. etc. (I, 169-170)

It is further embellished by a considerable quantity of that ambling lachrymose verse which one associates with the pages of *The Keepsake:* —

> The skies were its birth-place — the TEAR was the child
> Of the dark maiden SORROW, by young JOY beguiled;
> It was born in convulsion; 'twas nurtur'd in woe;
> And the world was yet young when it wander'd below. (II, 190)

There is some excuse for all this. Though published fourteen months later than the *Memoirs, Antonina* was conceived and begun much earlier. For the *Memoirs,* the young author had probably no model, unless it was Boswell's *Johnson,* for *Antonina,* such models as he had were bad, with a kind of badness peculiarly tempting to the mind of youth; in undertaking the *Memoirs,* he set out with a modest appreciation of the difficulties of his task,[10] whereas, with *Antonina,* he

---

[10] "This undertaking, though in appearance simple, combines among its requirements so much justice in the appreciation of character, and so much discrimination in the selection of examples, that its difficulties have been felt by the greatest as by the humblest intellects that have approached it. A task thus experienced as arduous, by all who have attempted it, must present a double responsibility when the office of biographer is assumed by a son.... Feeling the difficulty and delicacy of the employment on which I am about to venture," etc. (*Memoirs,* I, 1-2).

felt his foot to be upon the first rung of the ladder of fame, and began with a bold rebuke to his predecessors in the realm of historic fiction and a confident determination to show them how the thing ought to be done. In his preface he, by implication, deprecates the methods of those who select heroes and heroines from the real personages of the period, observing with considerable truth, and no doubt with an admonitory eye on Sir Walter Scott and Harrison Ainsworth, that this procedure leads to "confusing or falsifying dates . . . ."[11] He writes the word "Rome" as the heading to his third chapter, and then hastens to assure us that this title need excite no apprehensions "in the breasts of experienced readers".

> They will doubtless imagine that it is portentous of long rhapsodies on those wonders of antiquity, the description of which has long since become absolutely nauseous to them by incessant iteration. They will foresee wailings over the Palace of the Caesars, and meditations among the arches of the Colosseum, loading a long series of weary paragraphs to the very chapter's end . . . . we hasten to assure them, that in no instance will the localities of our story trench upon the limits of the well-worn Forum, or mount the arches of the exhausted Colosseum. It is with the beings, and not the buildings of old Rome, that their attention is to be occupied. We desire to present them with a picture of the inmost emotions of the times, — of the living, breathing, actions and passions of the people of the doomed Empire. (I, 91-92)

The programme was am ambitious one, and all that can be said is that Wilkie Collins was not the right man to carry it out. The historical facts are there, but not the historical sense; Goths and Romans alike hail from Wardour Street; the fifth-century Christians are nineteenth-century Protestants; the stock villain, virgin, and fanatic utter the stock sentiments appropriate to villainy, virginity, and fanaticism.

This was not the unanimous verdict of contemporary criticism. The *Athenaeum,* with an enthusiasm which seems exaggerated, hailed the rising of a new first-magnitude star: —

> a richly-coloured impassioned story, busy with life, importunately strong in its appeals to our sympathy — one which claims rank not far behind the antique fictions of Lockhart, Croly, Bulwer and Ward. Mr. Collins is possibly less deeply scholastic, less precisely

---

[11] I, x. The preface to the 1865 edn. is considerably condensed from the earlier, and more dogmatic in tone.

antiquarian than many of his predecessors; but his dramatic instinct makes up for want of elaborate training. Goth and Roman, Christian and Pagan are contrasted by him with a power which no closet study can give. In their vitality we have a glimmer of that burning breathing life which the Warwickshire deer-stealer could throw into his *Cleopatra,* and *Cressida,* and *Coriolanus,* and *Brutus.*[12]

One phrase of this eulogy is justified: the dramatic instinct is there, though uncertain and crude in its manifestations. And there is something more. Faint and gasping beneath the historical trappings, the author of *The Woman in White* is already struggling into view. He is dimly recognizable in the preface, declaring that it was "one main object of his anxety... to make his plot invariably arise, and proceed out of, the great historical events of the era, exactly in the order in which they occurred", and laying stress upon "all the various historical illustrations of the period which the Author's researches among conflicting but equally important authorities had enabled him to garner up" (I, x-xi). The passion for documentation, the confident appeal to historical fact, with which the sensation novelists of the century defended themselves against the charge of improbability are already present in the preface to *Antonina.* There are the accents of the same voice which in *Basil* protests: "I founded the main event out of which this story springs, on a fact in real life which had come within my own knowledge";[13] which called in "professional men" to witness the accuracy of the law, medicine and chemistry of *Armadale;* which in *Heart and Science* adduces the evidence of *The Times* and *Chambers' Encyclopaedia* in support of Mrs. Gallilee's researches into "the idea of atoms" and the "Diathermancy of Ebonite"; which cites the Report of the Royal Commission with reference to the marriage laws discussed in *Man and Wife;* which explains in the preface to *Jezebel's Daughter* "that the accessories of the scenes in the Deadhouse of Frankfort have been studied on the spot"; and which, in *Blind Love,* tells the story of the von Scheurer Insurance Fraud with hardly a detail

---

[12]*Athenaeum,* 16th March 1850, p. 285. Even after Collins' death in 1889, the *Biograph* committed itself to the remarkable opinion that: "Perhaps of all the works we have mentioned, that which shows the author to the best advantage as a student and a scholar is 'Antonina or The Fall of Rome'. It is full of character and fine work." But the phrase "as a student and a scholar" rather limits the application of this judgment.

[13](London: Richard Bentley, 1852), I, x.

changed. *Antonina* was not, of course, the first historical romance to boast of its fidelity to fact (though it certainly represented a wholesome reaction against the monstrous liberties taken by Harrison Ainsworth); its importance lies in showing the trend of Collins' mind. He was already preparing to become the father of modern detective fiction, with its insistence on scientific exactitude and the romance of accurate detail.

In *Antonina* also we have our first glimpse of Wilkie Collins the plot-maker. It is not particularly impressive and suggests no great originality, but, comparing the novel with its predecessors of the same class, we may notice a certain economy of incident and care to tuck in the ends of the threads, characteristic of the mature Collins. The central point, about which the whole story turns, is the opposition between Numerian, the fanatical Christian who lives to restore the primitive simplicity of the Faith, and Ulpius, the fanatical pagan who lives to restore the worship of the ancient gods. Numerian's fanaticism leads him to suspect his daughter Antonina of sin with the voluptuary Vetranio; he drives her from her home and she falls into the hands of the Goths. Here she is beloved by the young chieftain Hermanric and hated by Hermanric's fierce sister, Goisvintha. Ulpius' fanaticism leads him to betray Rome to the Goths and so bring about the reunion of all the characters in the sack of the city, when it turns out that Ulpius is really the long-lost brother of Numerian. Vetranio repents under the influence of Antonina's pure beauty; Goisvintha is killed by Ulpius, who goes mad and is burnt by the Christian priests. In this simple and symmetrical manner the rival fanaticisms of the two brothers provide the knot by which the history and the fiction are tied together. A number of highly-coloured melodramatic episodes give the story an appearance of complication which it does not, in fact, possess. Much the same thing might be said of *The Moonstone,* or, indeed of all Collins' best work, except, perhaps, *Armadale.* Compared with the plot of a modern thriller, the central intrigue is nearly always of massive simplicity; it is in the detail of the development that the elaboration occurs. In *Antonina,* the simplicity of conception stands out the more clearly because there are practically no subordinate characters, and no light and shade, the book being written throughout in a single key.

The conventionality of the characters is obvious: one thing only is of importance for the later Collins, and that is the contrast between Goisvintha and her brother Hermanric. Goisvintha's ferocious hunger for revenge on the Romans is the goad in her milder brother's side. She urges him on with harangues and reproaches and, when he is weak enough to spare Antonina, she cuts the sinews of his wrists and delivers him over to the Huns. Here, in Collins' first novel, we already have the two characters whom he reproduced so often, and so much more convincingly, in his later books: the weak and amiable man, set over against the strong, masculine, domineering woman, eaten up with the passion to be and do.

Antonina abounds in purple passages of description. With what youthful zest does the author let himself go upon the drunken orgy of Vetranio's "banquet of famine", with its riot of lamps and rich hangings, luxurious couches, scented oils, and gold and ivory ornaments, the repulsive "mash" of boiled bran and salted horseflesh set before the famine-stricken guests, the howling mob outside and the hideous corpse brought in to preside over the feast! With what exuberance does he gloat upon the sack of the city, the madness of Ulpius, the burning of the Temple! What fun he has with the murderous mechanical booby-trap into which Ulpius lures Goisvintha to her death! Better than these is the description of Ulpius, delirious with wounds, creeping through the secret breach in the walls of Rome to deliver the city to Alaric. There is action, though the execution is still clumsy, and there is always the artist's power of visualizing a scene in form and colour.

From time to time, indeed, the artist's hand is only too apparent. There are scenes which are purely static compositions — passages which read, not like a description of the thing itself, but like the catalogue description of a canvas:

> Near a confused mass of weapons, scattered on the ground, reclined a group of warriors apparently listening to the low, muttered conversation of three men of great age, who rose above them, seated on pieces of rock, and whose long, white hair, rough skin dresses, and lean tottering forms, appeared in strong contrast

with the iron-clad and gigantic figures of their auditors beneath. Above the old men, on the high road, was one of Alaric's waggons; and on the heaps of baggage piled against its clumsy wheels, had been chosen the resting-place of the future conqueror of Rome. The top of the vehicle seemed absolutely teeming with a living burden. Perched in every available nook and corner, were women and children of all ages, and weapons and live stock of all varieties. Now, a child — lively, mischievous, inquisitive — peered forth over the head of a battering ram. Now, a lean, hungry sheep, advanced his inquiring nostrils sadly to the open air; and displayed by the movement, the head of a withered old woman, pillowed on his woolly flanks. Here, appeared a young girl, struggling half entombed in shields. There, gasped an emaciated camp-follower, nearly suffocated in heaps of furs. The whole scene . . . presented . . . a gloomy conjunction of the menacing and the sublime. (I, 17-19)

From the débris carefully disposed to fill up the foreground to the woods and mists of the background, the entire scene, with its miscellaneous figures grouped about the infant "future conqueror of Rome" strongly calls to mind one of those vast "historical compositions", rather over-oily in texture and rather brown in the shadows, which the artist of the day was expected to produce for the Academy.

This is hardly surprising. The *Memoirs* had abounded in just such descriptions of canvases, and no doubt this style of writing had become a habit.[14] Moreover, Wilkie himself was still not quite certain of his own vocation. In 1849 — the year in which *Antonina* was completed — he had contributed a landscape to the Academy exhibition. It seemed possible that he might yet be a painter like his father. Painting was so much in the family, after all. Charley, who had entered the Royal Academy School as a student at the age of fifteen, was already an established artist, closely associated and in sympathy with the Pre-Raphaelite movement, though he never was made a full Brother. Mrs. Collins, who, after her husband's death had resided for about two years at 38 Blandford Square,[15] had moved in 1849 to 17 Hanover Terrace, Regent's Park. Wherever she went, her house became a gathering-place for artists and

---

[14]In the original preface, Collins speaks frankly from the painter's point of view: 'By this plan, it was thought . . . that, in the painter's phrase, the "effects" might thus be best "massed," and the "lights and shadows" most harmoniously "balanced" and "discriminated" ' (I, xii).

[15]Described under the name of "Baregrove Square" in *Hide and Seek* (Ellis, p. 13).

their friends; she gave "evenings", over which she presided with unending geniality and an obliging tolerance of tobacco-smoke in the drawing-room. Here, any day in the week, one might find the Wards, the Rossettis, William Frith, or Augustus Egg, besides Millais and Holman Hunt, who were intimate friends of Charley Collins. Indeed, the artistic atmosphere at the Collins' house must have been hard to escape; Mr. S. M. Ellis, indeed, thinks that the pressure of the family environment, "where it was taken for granted that he would be a great painter", did much to thrust the delicate and sensitive Charley into a path which he was not temperamentally equipped to follow. "I took to drawing from mere habit", he confessed later, "and they all applauded my efforts. I looked upon the diadem as a part of manhood that must come, and now I begin to doubt and fear the issue".[16] Wilkie was made of sterner stuff than his brother, but it was impossible that he should altogether escape the influence of his surroundings. Of his Academy landscape all trace seems now to be lost. It hung for many years in his study, and Holman Hunt tells how, if the visitor's eye strayed to it, he would burst out: "Ah! you might well admire that masterpiece; it was done by that great painter Wilkie Collins, and it put him so completely at the head of landscape painters that he determined to retire from the profession in compassion from the rest. The Royal Academy were so affected by its supreme excellence and its capacity to teach, that they carefully avoided putting it where taller people in front might obscure the view, but instead placed it high up, that all the world could without difficulty survey it. Admire, I beg you, sir, the way in which those colours stand; no cracking in that *chef d'oeuvre,* and no tones ever fail. Admire the brilliancy of that lake reflecting the azure sky; well, sir, the painter of that picture has no petty jealousies, that unrivalled tone was compounded simply with Prussian blue and flake white, it was put on you say by a master hand, yes but it will show what simple materials in such a hand will achieve. I wish all masterpieces had defied time so triumphantly" (*Pre-Raphaelitism* II, 186-187). There was perhaps a dig here at Hunt and his cherished "mystery" of working transparent colour over a foundation of

---

[16]Ellis, pp. 57-58. Collins' confession is quoted from Hunt's *Pre-Raphaelitism,* I, 298.

wet white. The masterpiece was probably sold at his death with the rest of his household property.

Antonina was favourably received on the whole. Though it achieved no very great sale it did something to increase the author's fame. We find him attending a civic banquet, where he was mistaken for his Pre-Raphaelite brother and asked "whether the author of *Antonina* was there that night".[17] His next enterprise, however, was not after the high Roman fashion. By way of relaxation from his studies, he went, during the summer and autumn of 1850, for a walking-tour in Cornwall, accompanied by his friend Henry C. Brandling, the artist. The sequel to this was *Rambles beyond Railways*,[18] written during the winter of 1850 and published in January 1851, with some attractive lithographs by Brandling.

As a fresh and easily-written piece of journalism, the *Rambles* would be hard to beat. It makes no pretentions to antiquarian learning — the famous "Furry dance" is dismissed with banter as an "extraordinary absurdity" — but a good many quaint customs and traditions are described and excellent popular accounts are given of the pilchard fisheries and the mines, and of some of the local curiosities such as the Cheese-Wring and Hurlers at Liskeard, the Loggan Stone at Trereen and the cutting of the sand-bar at Loo Pool. In 1850, Cornwall was literally "beyond railways" though the iron road was driven through little more than a year afterwards, and Collins and his companion with their knapsacks were frequently mistaken for "mappers", plotting out the course of the line. The people were still primitive; relics of the old Cornish tongue still lingered among them, making their speech difficult for the travelers to understand; a couple of tourists, foot-slogging for their own pleasure was a phenomenon unknown and almost unbelievable. But the modern spirit had already begun to penetrate even these wilds: one of the most entertaining chapters in the book describes "the beautiful drama of The Curate's Daughter" as enacted at the "unrivalled Sans Pareil Theatre" at Redruth; a performance which Collins regretfully

---

[17]Letter to E. M. Ward, quoted in Ellis, p. 13.
[18]*Rambles beyond Railways; or, Notes in Cornwall Taken A-Foot.* By W. Wilkie Collins, author of The "Life of William Collins, R. A.;" "Antonina," & c. London: Richard Bentley, 1851.

compares with what must have been the charm of the ancient Cornish miracle plays given in the amphitheatre at Piran Round. In the comparison he shows a taste and humour which make up for his derisory attitude to the Furry Dance. The author's description of himself, as he appeared when descending the Botallack Mine in the clothes provided for him by the miners, makes a charming companion-picture to Millais' stately portrait of the same date, and gives a good idea of the light, gossiping style of the book: —

> The same mysterious dispensation of fate, which always awards tall wives to short men, decreed that a suit of the big miner's should be reserved for me. He stood six feet two inches — I stand five feet six inches. I put on his flannel shirt — it fell down to my toes, like a bedgown; his drawers — and they flowed in Turkish luxuriance over my feet. At his trousers I helplessly stopped short, lost in the voluminous recesses of each leg. The big miner, like a good Samaritan as he was, came to my assistance. He put the pocket button through the waist button-hole, to keep the trousers up in the first instance; then, he "hauled taught" the braces (as the sailors say) until my waistband was under my armpits; and then he pronounced that I and my trousers fitted each other in great perfection. The cuffs of the jacket were next turned up to my elbows — the white nightcap was dragged over my ears — the round hat was jammed down over my eyes. When I add to all this, that I am so near-sighted as to be obliged to wear spectacles, and that I finished my toilette by putting my spectacles on (knowing that I should see little or nothing without them) nobody, I think, will be astonished to hear that my companion seized his sketch-book, and caricatured me on the spot; and that the grave miner, polite as he was, shook with internal laughter, as I took up my tallow-candles and reported myself ready for a descent into the mine.
>
> (Pages 206-207)

The descriptions of landscape are, as usual, good; they are expressed with more freedom and less straining after the sublimity than the "set pieces" of *Antonina,* and Collins can always be relied on for an apt descriptive touch, as when he likens the great slabs of fish hung up to dry on the cottage walls to the "legs of many dirty duck trousers", or notes that, in the still seclusion of the Vale of Mawgan, "the dull fall of the latch, when an idle child carelessly opens the church-yard wicket, sounds from one end of the village to the other."

So far, Wilkie Collins' literary achievements, though not unsuccessful, had been tentative and miscellaneous — an essay in biography, an attempt at the historical novel, a little excursion into journalism. But in the following year he was to come under a new influence, the most important in his whole career, which was to establish him definitely as a professional man of letters and lead him into that way which he was to make peculiarly his own.

HERMANRIC PROTECTS ANTONINA FROM THE FIERCE GOISVINTHA

CHAPTER IV

Among the favorite amusements of the young Collinses when living at 38 Blandford Square were amateur theatricals. Wilkie and E. M. Ward (who was then living just round the corner at 33 Harewood Square) were especially active in these productions, bringing off, among others, quite elaborate performances of *The Good-Natured Man* and *The Rivals*.[1] Accordingly, when, on 8th March 1851, Charles Dickens was looking for some one to play Smart in Bulwer's *Not So Bad as We Seem* — "a small part, but, what there is of it, decidely good"[2] — he recalled to mind that Augustus Egg had mentioned Wilkie Collins as a young man who would be only too delighted to play any thing for them, and wrote off to Egg:

> Will you undertake to ask him if I shall cast him in this part? If yes, I will call him to the reading on Wednesday; have the pleasure of leaving my card for him (say where), and beg him to favour us with his company at dinner on Wednesday evening. I knew his father well, and should be very glad to know him. (Pages 7-8)

Dickens was thirty-nine years old and at the very height of his powers and fame. He was brilliant; he dazzled; and if the unhappy restlessness which ultimately devoured him was already at work upon him, it showed itself as yet only as a magnificent energy. In the previous year he had finished *Copperfield,* inaugurated *Household Words* and flung himself eagerly into the new enterprise of the *Guild of Literature and Art.* The Guild was a disappointment, but the theatrical performances which were to raise money for it provided all the fun and excitement for which he craved. Wilkie Collins was at once caught up into the swing of things. Dickens seems to have taken an immediate fancy to him, and even John Forster, jealous of the younger man's influence, was forced to admit that, from this time forward, "Mr. Wilkie Collins became, for all

---

[1] Stewart M. Ellis, *Wilkie Collins, Le Fanu, and Others* (London: Constable, 1931), pp. 12-13.
[2] *Letters of Charles Dickens to Wilkie Collins,* ed. Laurence Hutton (New York: Harper, 1892), p. 7, hereafter cited as *Letters* to differentiate it from the *Letters of Charles Dickens,* 2d edn. (London: Macmillan, 1893), quoted below.

the rest of the life of Dickens, one of his dearest and most valued friends".[3] On 12 May 1851, we find Dickens replying to the request of "My dear Collins"[4] for an invitation for the first performance of the play and to the supper given afterwards by the Duke of Devonshire:

> Under these circumstances, I feel the introduction of a stranger like Mr. Ward's brother ... a kind of difficulty; but I do not like to refuse compliance with any wish of my faithful and attached valet[5] whom I greatly esteem. I therefore merely mention this and send him the order. (*Letters*, p. 9)

The 16 May was the day of the performance at Devonshire House, and there "in the presence of Her Majesty the Queen and His Royal Highness the Prince Albert", Mr. Wilkie Collins made his first appearance on any public stage, in company with Douglas Jerrold, Dudley Costello, John Forster, Mark Lemon, John Tenniel, Frank Stone and other notables and notables-to-be. Dickens wrote to Forster: "You have no idea how good Tenniel, Topham, and Collins have been in what they had to do" (*Life*, p. 520). In subsequent performances at the Hanover Square Rooms, and when the company went on tour in the following year, the old "petite comedy" *Used Up* and the new farce by Dickens and Lemon, *Mr. Nightingale's Diary* were added to the repertory, Collins taking, in the former the part of "James" and, in the latter, that of "Lithers, the landlord of the Water Lily."

The first literary fruit of this association was, as might be expected, a frankly Dickensian imitation: a little Christmas tale entitled *Mr. Wray's Cash-Box,* which was published in book form in January 1852, with a delicately etched frontispiece by Millais.[6] The "mystery", which is not a very profound one, is cleared up in Chapter 4, having been previously given away in the preface, and the story is, as the author himself says, "a simple story, simply and familiarly told ... as if I were only telling it to an audience of friends at my own fireside"

---

[3] *The Life of Charles Dickens,* ed. J. W. T. Ley (London: Cecil Palmer, 1928), p. 520.
[4] Collins remained "My dear Collins" till after the "Lazy Tour" to Cumberland, when he became "My dear Wilkie."
[5] Dickens played the part of Lord Wilmot, the employer of Smart.
[6] *Mr. Wray's Cash-box;* or The Mask and the Mystery. A Christmas Sketch. By W. Wilkie Collins, author of *Antonina,* etc. etc. Bentley 1852.

(p. vi). There is a virtuous old actor, a gentle and virtuous maiden, a ludicrous and devoted attendant, who eventually marries the virtuous maiden, and so forth, and a tone of mild pleasantry alternates with one of gentle pathos throughout. The little tale is of no great importance, except that it shows Wilkie Collins making his first real attempt to depict character, and marks, on the whole a distinct advance toward a workmanlike simplicity of style. The simplicity is still very self-conscious, and the narrative is disfigured by those apostrophes to, and buttonholings of, the reader, of which Collins never completely freed himself, any more than did Trollope or Thackeray.

> Allow me to introduce him to you: — THE GENTLE READER — JULIUS CAESAR. Stop! start not at those classic syllables; I will explain all. (Page 33)

There are passages of laboured facetiousness, produced in deference to the taste of the time and always handled, by Collins, with an elephantine lack of grace or taste: —

> He knocked down a salt-cellar, spirted some gravy over his shirt; and spilt a potato, in trying to transport it a distance of about four inches, from the dish to Anne's plate. (Page 102)

But there are also touches of the genuine Collins humour, which is purely satiric: —

> As a genteel provincial residence, who is unacquainted with it? The magnificent new Hotel that has grown on to the side of the old Inn; the extensive Library, to which, not satisfied with only adding new books, they are now adding a new entrance as well; the projected Crescent of palatial abodes in the Grecian style, on the top of the hill, to rival the completed Crescent of castellated abodes, in the Gothic style, at the bottom of the hill—are not such local objects as these perfectly well known to any intelligent Englishman? (Pages 1-2)

The principal character, that of an old actor of the usual pathetic type, with a mania for Shakespeare and Kemble, doubtless grew out of Collins' pre-occupation at the time with theatricals. We note also the preface, giving chapter and verse for the origin of the plot, and the two footnotes on p. 19: "A fact! See Boaden's Life of Kemble, vol. i. p. 326" — "Another fact!!

See the same work, vol. i. p. 256" — as evidence of the ruling passion for documentation.

In November 1851, Wilkie Collins brought his legal career to an honorable conclusion: —

> 17. Hanover Terrace
> Regents Park
> Monday evening.
>
> Dear Henry, The affecting national ceremony of calling me to the Bar, will take place on Friday next (21st). If you dont mind Lincoln's Inn wine, and have no better engagement, it will give me great pleasure to see you at the Call Party.
>
> Very faithfully yours
> W. Wilkie Collins
>
> To Thomas Joseph Henry, Esqre.[7]

So far as is known, Collins never made any attempt to practise his nominal profession. Literature was henceforward to be his true vocation, and he was already well advanced upon something very much more important than *Mr. Wray's Cash-Box* and altogether unlike it; something, in fact, so entirely different from anything written by him before or since, that we cannot help wondering what kind of greatness Collins might conceivably have attained had the spirit of the time, the influence of Dickens and the as yet unsuspected growth in himself of a new kind of talent allowed him to continue his development in this direction.

Basil[8] was heralded into the world by a lengthy and pretentious preface, in the form of a dedicatory letter to Charles James Ward, which might well serve as a manifesto for the whole school of "sensation fiction". It almost merits, one feels, to have become as much a *locus classicus* as the preface to *Bérénice*.

Collins begins by explaining, more eloquently than convincingly why he does not intend to follow up the success of *Antonina* by another classical romance:

---

[7][Letter transcribed from Miss Sayers' copy, not the original, now in the H. R. C. Ed.]]
[8]*Basil: A Story of Modern Life*. By W. Wilkie Collins, Author of "Antonina," "Rambles Beyond Railways," etc. etc. In Three Volumes. London: Richard Bentley, New Burlington Street. 1852.

> I could not find, in Ancient History, any second subject which, to *my* judgment offered itself so perfectly to all the requirements of romance, as the subject I was fortunate enough to find for "ANTONINA." On that account, therefore, I abandoned the idea of building my second work on a classical foundation. (I, vii)

Having thus dismissed the ancient world, he toys for a moment with the notion of a subject taken from Modern History, and continues:

> the temptation of trying if I could not successfully address myself, at once, to the readiest sympathies and the largest number of readers, by writing a story of our own times, was too much for me. So I wrote this book. (I, viii)

Here he ranges himself, once and for all, on the side of those writers who unashamedly set out to please the great public and accept the world's judgment. Like Dickens, he wrote for the common man and not for the literary critic and valued his work according to the favour it found with the contemporary public. If the world is to be divided into high-brows and low-brows, Collins was a low-brow unqualified. He studied to please and was proud to do so. Reade, abandoning historical romance for contemporary melodrama, threw the new venture to the world like a bone to a dog. "I write for the public, and the public don't care about the dead. They are more interested in the great tragicomedy of humanity that is around and about them and environs them at every crossing, in every hole and every corner. An aristocratic divorce suit, the last great social scandal, a sensational suicide from Waterloo Bridge, a woman murdered in Seven Dials, or a baby found strangled in a bandbox at Piccadilly Circus interests them more than Margaret's piety or Gerard's journey to Rome. . . . The paying public prefers a live ass to a dead lion."[9] But Collins was one with his public.

He was anxious, however, to make it clear that his new venture demanded as much art and craftsmanship as the old.

> Industry in collecting useful information; discretion in selecting it;

---

[9] [Miss Sayers placed a footnote number in her text, but neglected to put in the note itself. Reade's statement was originally quoted by John Coleman in *Charles Reade as I Knew Him* (London: Treherne, 1903), pp. 263-264, and later picked up by Walter C. Phillips in *Dickens, Reade, and Collins: Sensation Novelists* (New York: Columbia Univ. Press, 1919), pp. 126-127. Since Miss Sayers included Phillips' book in a list of Collins materials that she prepared around 1928, he was probably her source. The list is in a notebook now at Wheaton College. Ed.]

and care and intelligence in using it, were just as important in the one case, as in the other. The difference was in the *quality* of the knowledge required, not in the *quantity:* and the difficulty of employing that knowledge successfully when I had got it, was tenfold greater in the new task than in the old. When I was writing about the people of the fifth century to the people of the nineteenth, many and many an error might be expected to pass unnoticed: when I was writing *of* the people of our own times, *to* the people of our own times, what single error, what misappreciation even, could hope to escape? (I, ix-x)

And he proceeds to enunciate his literary creed:

> Fancy and Imagination, Grace and Beauty, all those qualities which are to the work of Art what scent and colour are to the flower, can only grow toward Heaven by taking root in earth. After all, is not the noblest poetry of prose fiction the poetry of every-day truth? (I,xi)

This is, in substance, the same formula which was summed up by Reade as "matter-of-fact Romance"[10] and by Dickens, in the preface to *Bleak House* as, "the romantic side of familiar things".

Collins continues in words which, *mutatis mutandis,* voice the doctrine of his friends the Pre-Raphaelites:

> Directing my characters and my story, then, towards the light of Reality wherever I could find it, I have not hesitated to violate some of the sentimental conventionalities of sentimental fiction. For instance, the first love-meeting of two of the personages in this book, occurs ... in the very last place [an omnibus], and under the very last circumstances which the artifices of sentimental writing would sanction .... So again, in certain parts of this book where I have attempted to excite the suspense or pity of the reader, I have admitted as perfectly fit accessories to the scene the most ordinary street-sounds that could occur, at the time and in the place represented — believing that by adding to truth, they were adding to tragedy .... (I, xi-xii)

Then comes his central theory of the Novel, in a passage which incidentally lays bare the secret of his own astonishing technique: —

> Believing that the Novel and the Play are twin-sisters in the

---

[10]Preface to *Hard Cash.*

family of Fiction; that the one is a drama narrated, as the other is a drama acted; and that all the strong and deep emotions which the Play-writer is privileged to excite, the Novel-writer is privileged to excite also, I have not thought it either politic or necessary, while adhering to realities, to adhere to common-place, everyday realities only. In other words, I have not stooped so low as to assure myself of the reader's belief in the probability of my story, by never once calling on him for the exercise of his faith. Those extraordinary accidents and events which happen to few men, seemed to me as legitimate materials for fiction to work with, when there was a good object in using them, as the ordinary accidents and events which may, and do, happen to us all. By appealing to genuine sources of interest *within* the reader's own experience, I could certainly gain his attention to begin with; but it would be only by appealing to other sources (as genuine in their way) *beyond* his own experience, that I could hope to fix his interest and excite his suspense, to occupy his feelings, or to stir his thoughts. (I, xiii-xiv)

The theory is no new one: it is that of Corneille: « Je ne craindrai pas d'avancer que le sujet d'une belle tragédie doit n'être pas vraisemblable », which saying Lanson interprets in exactly the same sense and almost exactly the same words as Collins: "il entend par là que les évenements qui arrivent tous les jours, qui n'excitent aucune surprise, ne sont pas ceux que la tragédie doit choisir. Il faut qu'on s'étonne du fait, pour que l'on prenne un vif plaisir à voir comment c'est arrivé.[11] And to Corneille also, the aim of Art was to please: "La poésie dramatique a pour but le seul plaisir du spectateur".[12] The quarrel between the sensational and the unsensational is, indeed, a perennial one; at the moment when *Basil* appeared, it was entering upon a particularly savage and close-fought engagement on the terrain of the novel. Both sides, as always in any literary dispute, claimed to be fighting in the cause of reality and truth to nature. As always, the anti-sensationalists accused the sensationalists of extravagance and of pandering to the basest instincts of the mob, while the sensationalists, consciously or unconsciously following in the footsteps of their

---

[11]Gustave Lanson, *Corneille,* 4th edn. (Paris: Librairie Hachette, 1913), p. 68. [Corneille states: "I shall not hesitate to assert that the subject of a beautiful tragedy does not have to be plausible" ("Au Lecteur," *Héraclius*). This Lanson interprets in the following way: "He means by this that the events which happen every day, which excite no surprise are not those that tragedy ought to choose. One has to be surprised by the event in order to take real pleasure in finding out how it came about." Ed.]

[12][Lanson, p. 62: "The sole purpose of dramatic poetry is the pleasure of the spectator" *(Discours de l'utilité et des parties du poème dramatique).* Ed.]

first spokesman, Aristotle, retorted that these things really happened and that it is good to purge the emotions by pity and terror; adding, acidly, that it is better to be shocking than to be dull, and, if art is to be as pointless and tedious as real life, where is the use of it?

Three results naturally follow from the sensationalists' attitude. First, the more incredible the incidents they narrate, the more insistent they become that their narratives are founded in fact. "That which has happened", says Aristotle, "is manifestly possible, else it would not have come to pass."[13] Thus Reade has his note-books crammed with newspaper cuttings; thus Collins in his footnotes cries "A fact!" and adduces historical instances and technical opinions; and thus even Dickens, who disapproved of apologetic prefaces and declared that a book should stand upon its own legs,[14] was seduced, first into recounting the death of Krooke by spontaneous combustion and then, influenced perhaps by the anxious scrupulosity of Collins, into backing up the outrageous improbability by medical records.[15]

Secondly, in order, as Collins says, to gain the reader's attention in the first place, and in order to secure his belief in far more astonishing parts of the narrative, the sensationalist, if he knows his business, will strive for the utmost and most exact realism in the details of everything that happens "within the reader's own experience." Only then will he establish that "will to believe" which will predispose the reader to accept the apparently incredible. How easily the will to believe may be shattered and dispersed is shown by the indignation with which readers of any modern detective story will pounce upon the most trifling inaccuracy. Arnold Bennett declared that he was unable to put any faith in Mr. J. J. Connington's story *The Case with Nine Solutions,* because his confidence was

---

[13] *Poetics,* Ch. ix. [Miss Sayers used the trans. of Ingram Bywater (Oxford: Clarendon Press, 1929). Her copy, which is in the possession of Anthony Fleming, contains her pencilled annotations to the text. This passage is marked: "Stories founded on real facts." Ed.]

[14] "I think the probabilities here and there require a little more respect than you are disposed to show them, and I have no doubt that the prefatory letter would have been better away, on the ground that a book (of all things) should speak for and explain itself." Thus Dickens to Collins in a letter on the subject of *Basil,* 20th December 1852 (*Letters of Charles Dickens,* p. 281).

[15] *Bleak House,* [Pref. and Ch. xxxiii. Ed.]

destroyed at the start by an unimportant technical slip about a telephone-bell.[16] In the art of capturing confidence by this preliminary establishing of a reputation for accuracy, Collins was to prove himself a past-master.

In the third place, the sensationalist, having to defend himself against the charge of producing cheap and nasty effects, is obliged always to lay particular stress upon his status as a genuine artist. "Call me nasty if you will", he says in effect, "but you must not call me cheap. I have had to work like a horse to produce these effects you think so easy. I take my Art as seriously as any highbrow, and it is none the less Art because it pleases the man in the street." And thus the paragraph in the preface to *Basil* which follows immediately upon the statement of Collins' theory of the Novel is a belligerent attack upon "the mob of ladies and gentlemen who play at writing."

> There can be no literary man, I think, with the smallest respect for his vocation or for himself ... but must feel that this first, great merit of "painstaking" has now become doubly a merit in the present state of "light literature," as it is termed, in England. (I, xv)

And Dickens approvingly comments:

> It is delightful to find throughout that you have taken great pains with it besides, and have "gone at it" with a perfect knowledge of the jolter-headedness of the conceited idiots who suppose that volumes are to be tossed off like pancakes, and that any writing can be done without the utmost application, the greatest patience, and the steadiest energy of which the writer is capable.
> *(Letters of Charles Dickens,* p. 281)

The most important and enduring outcome of this attention to the technique of sensational fiction was the appearance in English literature of the novel with a plot as closely-knit and logical as the plot of a classical drama. One has only to read pre-Collins sensational novels — the incoherent eighteenth-century "tale of terror", the rambling picaresque chronicles of the "Newgate novel", and even the early books of Dickens — to realise how great and how necessary this innovation was. It is not too much to say that, without the writers of this group, and particularly without

---

[16] ¶["I Take Up the Challenge of Detective Fiction Lovers," *Evening Standard* (London), 17th January 1929, reprinted in *Arnold Bennett: The* Evening Standard *Years,* ed. Andrew Mylett (London: Chatto and Windus, 1974), pp. 232-234. Ed.]

Collins, the English novel of intrigue would either never have developed at all, or would have developed much later and upon much narrower and more Gothic lines. In particular, the modern English detective story could never have risen to its present position of international supremacy. It was Collins, Dickens and Reade who firmly wedded the novel of plot to the novel of character and kept it in the main line of development of English prose fiction.

A fourth consequence of the quarrel between the sensationalists and the anti-sensationalists was more temporary and more detrimental. Accused of being, not only cheap, but nasty, they thought it necessary to lay claim to an exalted moral object. Even to-day, the thriller-writer is constantly accused of leading the young into bad ways, and is occasionally goaded into pointing out that, on the contrary, his is the only modern literary *genre* which consistently makes virtue more sympathetic than vice; but his self-defense is made light-heartedly, and with his tongue in his cheek. Nobody seriously supposes that Mr. Henry Wade is sapping the foundations of society because his murderer escapes justice in *The Verdict of You All*.[17] But during the 'fifties, such accusations were seriously and passionately made, and could be extremely damaging. Accordingly, the preface to *Basil* concludes with a strenuous assertion of the book's moral usefulness: —

> Nobody who admits that the business of fiction is to exhibit human life, can deny that scenes of misery and crime must of necessity, while human nature remains what it is, form part of that exhibition — nobody can assert that such scenes are either useless or immoral in their effect on the reader, when they are turned to a plainly and purely moral purpose. (I, xvii-xviii)

Nevertheless, many people both could and did assert these things, with an emphasis which cowed even Wilkie Collins and which, though to the end of his life he protested against misconception, did undoubtedly influence and to some extent stunt the natural expression of his genius.

And now, what was the book that was thus loudly and elaborately trumpeted into the limelight?

---

[17][London: Constable, 1926. Ed.]

Basil is the story of a young man of aristocratic descent who falls in love at first sight with the daughter of a rich and vulgar linen-draper. He marries her privately, with the approval of her family, on the understanding that no cohabitation is to take place for a year, during which time he is to try and secure his father's consent to the match. On the night before that on which the marriage is to be consummated, the girl is seduced by her father's head-clerk. Basil discovers this and assaults the clerk, maiming him for life. This brings about an exposure of the whole sordid story. The girl dies of typhus and Basil, cast off by his father, retreats to a cottage in Cornwall to escape the vengeance of the clerk, who is eventually killed while attempting to murder him.

It will be seen that, judged by the standards of the time, this plot is moderately strong — not to say rancid. "I founded the main event," says Collins, "out of which this story springs, on a fact in real life which had come within my own knowledge: and in afterwards shaping the course of the narrative thus suggested, guided it as often as I could where I knew by my own experiences, and by the experiences incidentally related to me by others, that it would touch on something real and true, in its progress" (I, x-xi). This statement tells us little about the point at which fact ends and fancy begins. The fact that Basil himself is depicted as a young man engaged in writing a historical novel while studying for the Bar may lead us into speculations which, being unverifiable, are unprofitable. From internal evidence we can assert that the forcible-feeble ending, which concerns the vengeance of the villainous clerk, is crude and bad melodrama, unrelated to the facts of life; while everything that precedes it, including the seduction and the squalid financial bargaining with the heroine's father, bears the stamp of reality.[18] Even in this earlier part of the story there

---

[18]In this respect the book offers an interesting comparison with Disraeli's early novel *Vivian Grey,* and William F. Monypenny's remarks on the one work might be taken as a suggestive commentary upon the other: "In the earlier chapters especially we find the author writing from a genuine artistic impulse and with a joyous interest in his subject; and his story has all the coherence that comes from a strong and living conception of the character of the hero.... If we remember that *Vivian Grey* is only a work of fiction ... we may fairly say that in the first volume the hero is Disraeli himself; though just for that reason the work ought to have remained a fragment.... [In the second volume] signs of haste and discord at once begin to be apparent, and the remainder of the novel is a continuous descent. Both the narrative and the characters become incoherent.... Presently we lapse into vulgar and hideous melodrama.... It is just

are passages — such as those dealing with the fantastic family pride of Basil's father — in which the novelist has obviously stepped outside his own experience; but the central history of Basil's love-affair and its abominable ending is told with a kind of grim actuality which has little relation to anything in contemporary English fiction. It is a story of passion without sentiment, more French than English in its frank facing of sexual facts. "A domestic story of a somewhat repulsive kind", observed the *Daily News* in later years, "dealing as it did with a wife's infidelity with a sordid minuteness of detail which justly aroused a vigorous protest on the part of the critical journals" (obit., 24th September 1889). Needless to say, the modern reader who hastens to the book in the expectation of finding it another *Lady Chatterley's Lover* will be disappointed. There is not a word in it to which the most puritanical home secretary could take objection; while in the crushing punishment meted out to all offenders against the moral law, its morality is of the rigidest. What shocked the critics was, quite simply, the depiction of sexual passion unredeemed by romantic sentiment. Their condemnation angered Collins; he professed scorn for his critics; but he learned his lesson.[19] Not until *Armadale* did he attempt anything of the same kind again, and then only

---

such work as we might expect from a boy without experience who, in the reaction after a period of unnatural tension ending in great misfortune, is endeavouring in headlong haste to bring an earlier literary sketch to some sort of conclusion" (*The Life of Benjamin Disraeli, Earl of Beaconsfield*, I [London: John Murray, 1910], 90-91). The parallel is tempting, but it would be very unwise to read into *Basil* an autobiographical significance for which recorded facts offer only an unsubstantial basis.

[19]It has frequently been asserted in print that Collins lived to be ashamed of the "coarseness" of *Basil* and that, again to quote the *Daily News,* 24th September 1889, "He was accustomed to buy up and destroy a copy of the three-volume edition if it came in his way, and when, years afterwards, he prepared an edition in one volume for the press, the work was subjected to a laborious and, we may add, a by no means superfluous purification." Actually, any reader who takes the trouble to compare the editions of 1852 and 1862 will find that, with the exception of a sentence or so in Pt. I, Ch. viii containing the word "mistress", no "purgation" of the kind indicated has been attempted, the excisions being almost entirely undertaken in the interests of style and conciseness, as, for example, the tedious comic dialogue about the dog in Pt. I, Ch. vii and Basil's sentimental maunderings about his mother in Pt. I, Ch. ii. So far from being ashamed, Collins, in the preface to the new edition, stoutly defended the "purity" of his work: "Conscious of having designed and written my story with the strictest regard to true delicacy, as distinguished from false, I allowed the prurient misinterpretation of certain perfectly innocent passages in this book to assert itself as offensively as it pleased, without troubling myself to protest against an expression of opinion which aroused in me no other feeling than a feeling of contempt. I knew that 'Basil' had nothing to fear from pure-minded readers . . . . Slowly and surely, my story forced its way, through all adverse criticism, to a place in the public favor which it has never lost since . . . . All the indulgence I need now ask for 'Basil' is indulgence for literary defects . . . ."

with safeguards. *Basil* alone remains to show that it was in him to become, long in advance of his period, a frank exponent of physical passion.

Basil is a young man's book, crammed with errors and crudities, but it is a book that no one, looking for promise of future excellence, could disregard. The best word upon it has been said by Swinburne:

> violent and unlovely and unlikely as it is, this early story had in it something more than promise — the evidence of original and noticeable power to constrain and retain attention of a more serious and perhaps a more reasonable kind than can be evoked by many later and more ambitious and pretentious appeals to the same or a similar source of interest. The horrible heroine, beast as she is, is a credible and conceivable beast; and her hapless young husband is a rather pathetic if a rather incredible figure. But the vindictive paramour is somewhat too much of a stage property; and the book would hardly be remembered for better or for worse if the author had not in his future stories excelled its merits and eschewed its faults.[20]

The truth is that in *Basil* two Collinses were inharmoniously at work together. One of them — the Collins who was arrested in his development — was trying to write a realistic tale about a love-affair; the other, the Collins who was eventually to achieve greatness, was clumsily trying to put together a melodramatic plot about vengeance and horror. It was this second Collins who ruined the story and falsified its tone by making the wicked paramour a person with a long-cherished grievance against Basil's father, thus reducing the plain tale of passion to an unconvincing revenge-drama. The two elements are yoked but not mated together, and it is obvious that it is the "real" Collins — the "sensation" writer who here appears as the intruder upon Collins the realist.

But the book contains some extremely good things. There is the description of the rich linen-draper's brand-new villa in the dreary, half-built-over North-London suburb of "unfinished streets, unfinished crescents, unfinished squares, unfinished shops, unfinished gardens," a description which may have

---

[20]"Wilkie Collins," *Fortnightly Review*, 52 (1889), 590. [Swinburne's essay is reprinted in the Bonchurch edn. of *The Complete Works of Algernon Charles Swinburne*, XV (London: Heinemann, 1926), 289-306. Ed.]

been unconsciously in Dickens' mind when he wrote about the Veneerings.[21]

> Everything was oppressively new. The brilliantly-varnished door cracked with a report like a pistol when it was opened; the paper on the walls, with its gaudy pattern of birds, trellis-work, and flowers, in gold, red, and green on a white ground, looked hardly dry yet; the showy window-curtains of white and sky-blue, and the still showier carpet of red and yellow, seemed as if they had come out of the shop yesterday; the round rosewood table was in a painfully high state of polish; the morocco-bound picture books that lay on it, looked as if they had never been moved or opened since they had been bought; not one leaf even of the music on the piano was dogs-eared or worn. Never was a richly-furnished room more thoroughly comfortless than this — the eye ached at looking round it. There was no repose anywhere. The print of the Queen, hanging lonely on the wall, in its heavy gilt frame, with a large crown at the top, glared on you: the paper, the curtains, the carpet, glared on you: the books, the wax-flowers in glass-cases, the chairs in flaring chintz-covers, the china-plates on the door, the blue and pink glass vases and cups ranged on the chimney piece, the over-ornamented chiffoniers with Tonbridge toys and long-necked smelling bottles on their upper shelves, all glared on you. There was no look of shadow, shelter, secrecy, or retirement in any one nook or corner of those four gaudy walls. *All surrounding objects seemed startlingly near to the eye; much nearer than they really were.* (I, 198-200; Miss Sayers' italics)

The touch is a little over-emphatic, a little unsure here and there, but the ruthless accumulation of detail piles up to its effect, and the final touch is masterly.

In dialogue, Collins has found himself at last. The comic dialogue in the omnibus is overdone and was curtailed in later editions, and the scenes between Basil and his father and sister are high-falutin and unnatural, but the first interview of Basil with the linen-draper is admirable and so is the whole of his intercourse with the girl. Best of all, and probably most repulsive to Victorian sentiment, are the scenes in which Basil's brother Ralph appears. Ralph, the bad lad of the family, who has "contracted ... a reformatory attachment to a woman older than himself" and "devoted himself to collecting snuff-boxes and learning the violin" (I, 68-69) is the most successful character-sketch in the book; his cheerful worldli-

---

[21][In *Our Mutual Friend*. Ed.]

ness breaks in on Basil's stricken household like a breath of carbolic in an orchid-house.

> "The next question is about the girl," said my brother. "What's become of her? Where was she all the time of your illness?"
>
> "At her father's house: she is there still."
>
> "Ah, yes! I see: the old story — innocent, of course. And her father backs her, doesn't he? To be sure! that's the old story, too. I've got at our difficulty now: we are threatened with an exposure, if you don't acknowledge her. Wait a minute! Have you any evidence against her, besides your own?"
>
> "I have a letter, a long letter from her accomplice, containing a confession of his guilt and hers."
>
> "She's sure to call that confession a conspiracy. It's of no use to us, unless we dared to go to law — and we daren't: we must hush the thing up at any price; or it will be the death of my father. This is a case for money, just as I thought it would be. Mr. and Miss Shopkeeper have got a large assortment of silence to sell; and we must buy it of them, over the domestic counter, at so much a yard." (III, 97-98)

> "Give me the name and address . . . I shall ask my father for money for myself, and use as much of it as I think proper for your interests. He'll give me anything I want, now I've turned good boy. I don't owe fifty pounds, since my last debts were paid off — thanks to Madame, who is the most managing woman in the world. By the bye, when you see her, don't seem surprised at her being older than I am. Oh! this is the address, is it? Hollyoake Square? Where the devil's that? Never mind: I'll take a cab, and shift the responsibility of finding the place on the driver. (III, 103)

This has the authentic touch of nature, with its sly reference to the age of "the morganatic Mrs. Ralph" and its rallying but not unfeeling amusement at the younger brother's helpless innocence.[22] Equally delightful is Ralph's account of his interview with the blackmailing father:

> "I took him down, just as he swore his second oath. 'Sir,' said I, very politely, 'if you mean to make a cursing and a swearing conference of this, I think it only fair to inform you beforehand that you are likely to get the worst of it. When the whole repertory of British oaths is exhausted, I can swear fluently in five foreign languages; I have always made it a principle to pay back abuse at

---

[22][Miss Sayers' use of the phrase, "morganatic Mrs. Ralph," shows that she was referring to the 1862 or a later edn., since the 1852 edn. uses the word, *Madame,* instead. Ed.]

compound interest; and I don't exaggerate in saying, that I am quite capable of swearing you out of your senses, if you persist in setting me the example." (III, 119)

In a small way, Collins never did anything better than Ralph; he compensates for much that is inflated and absurd in this uneven but highly-promising novel.

The manuscript of *Basil* in the British Museum is written in an incredibly minute handwriting on the large square sheets which Collins seems always to have used. It is an early draft, offering many points of difference from the published edition, and is embellished here and there with marginal sketches and with specimen signatures in various forms of handwriting. One of these is an elaborate "W. Wilkie Collins" in imitation of the famous Dickens signature with the long flourish beneath. Evidently the author was studying the appearance of his title-pages, but the "W." did not disappear from his signature till after the publication of *Hide and Seek* in 1854. There are also a number of draft-titles, from which, and from the opening chapters of the story, we learn that the hero was originally called "Philip Lanreath."[23] A piece of comic cockney dialogue, in the forced and facetious style, between Basil and a tradesman's boy occurs in 〖Pt. I, Ch. v.〗 but was scrapped (wisely) before publication.

Of great interest in connection with Collins' orderly habits of working is a calendar at the end of Section VI, showing the progress of the novel, the various projected incidents in the story being assigned to certain days by numbers: —

		20th Sept.-1st. Vol.		
	Augt.	Augt.		
18.	Monday 34	25.................47		
19.	36	26.................49		
20.	38	27.................51	October	}
21.	40	28.................53	November	}
22.	42	29.................55		
23.	45	30.................60		

---

[23]〖Both here and at the end of the section discussing the ms. of *Basil,* Sayers indicated her desire to include an appendix. She also indicated that she wished facsimiles of the pages from *Basil* that she discusses included at the beginning of Chapter IV. The pages, which I reproduce, are difficult to decipher. One can presume that her appendix would have involved a lengthier discussion of the problems of the ms. Ed.〗

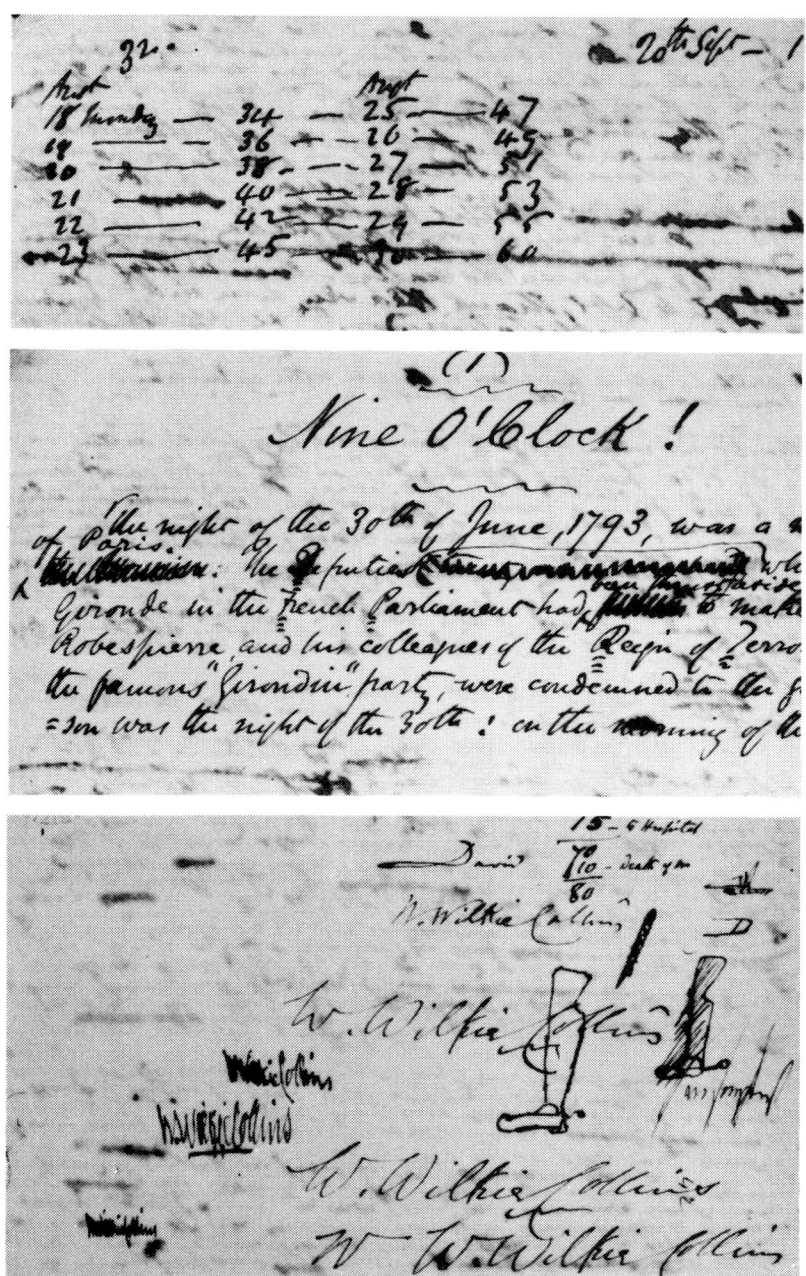

Pages from Manuscript of *Basil*.
Courtesy of British Library.

Apparently Collins was still Sabbatarian enough by training to avoid working on Sunday. A note further on elucidates the numbering: —

48. Letter	65. Death of Marg[aret]
50. Ralph	70. Ralph M[annion's] departure
55. Clara & Ralph	75. Cornwall — beginning of storm
60. Hospital & discovery	85. Last interview with M[annion] and end of journal Conclusion in letters

On the verso of several sheets are fragments of other literary efforts, including the head lines for one of a series of articles on "The Private Picture Galleries of England", the beginning of a sketch or tale about the French Revolution, entitled *Nine o'Clock!,* and the almost illegible notes of an article dealing with the Irish Exiles.

I have devoted considerable space to *Basil* because of its peculiar importance as a turning-point in Collins' literary career. It stands at the cross-roads where the Collins whom we know parts company from the Collins who might have been. Although it marks a steady progress towards achievement in the direction of plot and character construction, it yet remains as a rather melancholy monument — a citadel for ever unachieved.

Charles Dickens thought highly of it. In the letter already quoted he writes: "Not to play the sage or the critic (neither of which parts, I hope, is at all in my line), but to say what is the friendly truth, I may assure you that I have read the book with very great interest, and with a very thorough conviction that you have a call to this same art of fiction .... the story contains admirable writing, and many clear evidences of a very delicate discrimination of character .... I have made 'Basil's' acquaintance with great gratification, and entertain a high respect for him. And I hope that I shall become intimate with many worthy descendants of his, who are yet in the limbo of creatures waiting to be born" (*Letters of Charles Dickens,* p. 281).

The hope was fulfilled. No doubt Dickens already had his eye on Collins as a promising contributor to Household Words. But at the moment, Collins was chiefly delightful to him as a fresh and cheerful young companion, with whom he could escape from the over-faithful tutelage of Forster and the strained atmosphere of Tavistock House. He adds in a postscript:

> I am open to any proposal to go anywhere any day or days this week. Fresh air and change in any amount I am ready for. If I could only find an idle man (this is a general observation), he would find the warmest recognition in this direction.

It has been suggested, and perhaps with truth, that Collins' presence was not altogether welcome in the Dickens household, as tending to frivolity and dissipation. At the Collinses', on the other hand, Dickens was, naturally, an honoured guest. In April 1852, Millais writes to a friend:

> You ask me to describe the dance of Mrs. Collins .... It was a delightful evening. Charlie ... never got beyond a very solemn quadrille, though he is an excellent waltzer and polka dancer. Poor Mrs. C. was totally dumb from a violent influenza she unfortunately caught that very afternoon. She received all her guests in a whisper and a round face of welcome. There were many lions — amongst others the famous Dickens, who came for about half an hour and officiated as principal carver at supper.[24]

The solemn behaviour of Charlie Collins was probably the result of self-mortification; his High-Church piety was at this period excessive and a source of irritated amusement to the robuster Millais, with whom and with Holman Hunt he had been spending much time painting at Worcester Park Farm near Cheam. To Wilkie this asceticism was distasteful, both in itself and because he felt it to be bad for his brother's health. Timid, sensitive and self-critical, Charles Collins, for all his gifts and charm seems never to have succeeded in taking his rightful place in the world. He had already painted at least two pictures which had attracted favourable attention,[25] and was anxiously at work upon others; but his extreme self-distrust always stood in the way of his achievement. His unhappy

---

[24]John Guille Millais, *The Life and Letters of Sir John Everett Millais*, 2d edn. (London: Methuen, 1900), I, 163.
[25]"Convent Thoughts" 1851, "May in Regent's Park" 1852.

attachment to Maria Rossetti, who ended by renouncing the world for an Anglican sisterhood, increased the tendency to melancholy which probably sprang originally from a frail constitution. At this time Holman Hunt describes him as being "slight, with slender limbs, but erect in head and neck, and square in the shoulders ... having beautifully cut features, large chin, a crop of orange-coloured hair, and blue eyes that looked at a challenger without sign of quailing" (*Pre-Raphaelitism,* I, 293-294). Of the two brothers, Charles had undoubtedly the more attractive physical, and perhaps the finer mental, endowments; but he lacked the stiffness of fibre that makes for success. There is little record of close companionship between him and Wilkie, though they were affectionate brothers; among the brilliant band of writers and painters who gathered about the mother's hearth, Charles Collins seems to have passed like a gentle phantom, an "ineffectual angel", whose airy footprints left but little trace, whose frail wings, soon broken, beat the air in vain.

BASIL'S FATHER ORDERS HIM TO REMOVE HIS NAME FROM THE FAMILY BIBLE

CHAPTER V

Whatever may have been the secret history of storm and stress that underlay *Basil,* the next few years were the happiest and most care-free of Wilkie Collins' life. His friendship with Dickens grew apace, and their correspondence shows him to have been the great man's chosen companion in many a jaunt and ramble. On 23 December 1852, for example, Dickens writes: "if you will come there [i.e. to the *Household Words* office] tomorrow afternoon — say at about three o'clock — I think we may forage pleasantly for a dinner in the City, and then go and look at Christmas Eve in Whitechapel, which is always a curious thing."[1] On 18th January following, he is inviting Collins to join him on the Saturday evening and "revel in the glories of the eccentric British Drayma", and to partake of Gin Punch at "the Family Arms, Tavistock" on the Sunday. The idea of a trip to Italy is also under consideration:

> I have been thinking of the Italian project, and reducing the time to two months — from the 20th October to the 20th December — see the way to a trip that shall really not exclude any foremost place, and be reasonable too. (*Letters,* pp. 13-14)

Nor was Collins appreciated only as a play-fellow. The book upon which Dickens was then engaged was *Bleak House,* and we shall not be mistaken in tracing the influence of the younger writer in that increased elaboration of plot which here marks the beginning of Dickens' later period. It may also be significant that a considerable part of the book is written in the form of a personal "narrative", the very form which Collins was to make so peculiarly his own. Whether Collins suggested this, or whether, as is perhaps more likely, he merely saw the possibilities of the form and improved upon them later, is debatable; it is, however, certain that, for good or for ill, the mutual influence of the two writers began at this time and grew continually stronger in the years to come. Even without

---

[1] *Letters of Charles Dickens to Wilkie Collins,* ed. Laurence Hutton (New York: Harper, 1892), pp. 12-13, hereafter cited as *Letters* to differentiate it from the *Letters of Charles Dickens,* 2d edn. (London: Macmillan, 1893), quoted below.

Collins, it is likely that Dickens would have realised that the old-fashioned, loosely-knit, picaresque novel had had its day. No one knew better than he how to keep his finger on the public pulse. But it remains a fact that, starting from *Bleak House,* his plots grew steadily more closely-woven and more "Collinsian", until they ended in the impenetrable mystery of *Edwin Drood.*

It was about this time that Collins became acquainted with W. H. Wills, assistant-editor of *Household Words,* and with his wife's niece, Miss Chambers, who later married Frederick Lehmann, and to whom Collins wrote the only series of really intimate letters which have survived the years. A piece of verse addressed to Miss Chambers in 1852, apparently accompanied the gift of a toffee-apple. It explains itself, and shows that he could handle light verse with some address: —

> Miss Chambers has sent me a very sharp letter,
> With a gift of some Toffy (I never sucked better!).
> 'Tis plain, from her note, she would have me infer
> That *I* should have first sent the Toffy to *her.*
> I will only observe on the present occasion
> (Thinking first gifts of sweets so much sugar'd temptation),
> That, in tempting of all kinds, I still must believe
> The men act like Adam, the women like Eve.
> From mere mortal frailties I don't stand exempted,
> So I waited, like Adam, by Eve to be tempted;
> But, more fitted than he with 'The Woman' to grapple,
> I return her (in Toffy) my bite of 'the Apple.'[2]

In 1853 Collins is mentioned as a paid contributor in the office-book of *Household Words,* though his name did not make its appearance in the magazine itself until many years later, when it had already become too valuable an asset to be ignored. Dickens, who was firmly wedded to the principle of anonymous journalism for everybody except himself, gave no publicity to the names of his "young men" during the early time of struggle when it would have been of the greatest value to them, and announced the authorship of the serials in his magazines only when the authors were celebrated enough to demand it. In 1856, when Collins had already been writing for him for three years, and was growing a little restive under this treatment, Dickens blandly writes to Wills: —

---

[2]Rudolf Chambers Lehmann, *Memories of Half a Century* (London: Smith, Elder, 1908), p. 31.

> I observe that to a man in his [Collins'] position who is fighting to get on, the getting his name before the public is important. Some little compensation for its not being constantly announced is needed, and that I fancy might be afforded by *a certain engagement*.[3]

"Not being constantly announced" is admirable meiosis. This "certain engagement" was the transference of Collins to the permanent staff at the rate of five guineas a week, concerning which arrangement Dickens generously observes:

> [Collins] being industrious and reliable besides, I don't think we should be at an additional expense of £20 in the year by the transaction.

However, in 1853 Collins was no doubt eager enough to be published in *Household Words* on any conditions. The first story submitted seems to have been rejected by Dickens on account of its dealing with the subject of hereditary insanity and being therefore liable to pain "those numerous families in which there is such a taint." The story was probably an early draft of *Mad Monkton,* one of the finest of Collins' shorter tales, which afterwards appeared in *The Queen of Hearts*. Dickens, after deputing Wills to explain this point to Collins, adds (8 February 1853): —

> On the whole I am disposed to think that it will be best to accept his offer of a new story instead. And it is desirable to explain to him that a story within a story — as this is — is complicated and difficult for our peculiar purpose.
>
> I think there are many things, both in the inventive and descriptive way, that he could do for us if he would like to work in our direction. And I particularly wish him to understand this, and to have every possible assurance conveyed to him that I think so, and that I should particularly like to have his aid.
>
> (*Dickens as Editor,* p. 98)

Seeing that Dickens was in London at the time and living on intimate terms with Collins, one wonders why both the rejection and the encouragement should not have been communicated personally. Perhaps Dickens thought they would come with more official solemnity from a third party. In any case, the new story, *Gabriel's Marriage,* was duly

---

[3]Letter of 16th September, quoted in R. C. Lehmann, *Charles Dickens as Editor* (London: Smith, Elder, 1912), p. 221.

submitted and appeared in *Household Words* for April 16 and 23. The plot is the same which Collins afterwards worked into his play *The Lighthouse*. The story contains some fine, picturesque touches, and is the first in which Collins displays his mastery of the wild and weird. There are passages in it which remind us that Collins had Irish blood in him — passages with the wailing lilt of the writers of the Celtic Renaissance: —

> "The White Women! The White Women! Open the door, Gabriel! look out westward, where the ebb tide has left the sand dry. You'll see them bright as lightning in the darkness, mighty as the angels in stature, sweeping like the wind over the sea, in their long white garments, with their white hair trailing far behind them! Open the door, Gabriel! You'll see them stop and hover over the place where your father and your brother have been drowned; you'll see them come on till they reach the sand; you'll see them dig in it with their naked feet, and beckon awfully to the raging sea to give up its dead". [[7 (16th April 1853), 151]]

During these years also, Collins contributed to *Household Words* several other of the stories which were later collected under the title: *After Dark*. In February 1853, he wrote to his friend Ward that he was "overhead and ears in work", and a few months later actually confessed, "I blush to own that I shall be at work on Sunday!!!"[4]

The only blot upon the horizon was the ill-health which had already begun to dog him. In June 1853 Dickens writes from Boulogne:

> I hope you are as well as I am, and have as completely shaken off all your ailings. And I hope, too, that you are disposed for a long visit here.... You shall have a Pavilion room in the garden, with a delicious view, where you may write no end of Basils. You shall get up your Italian .... You shall live, with a delicate English graft upon the best French manner, and learn to get up early in the morning again. In short, you shall be thoroughly prepared, during the whole summer season, for those travels that are to come off anon. (*Letters*, pp. 14-15)

A week later he writes again, "I am very sorry indeed to hear so bad an account of your illness, and had no idea it had been so severe."

---

[4]Stewart M. Ellis, *Wilkie Collins, Le Fanu, and Others* (London: Constable, 1931), p. 16.

The trouble passed, however, and Collins paid his visit to Dickens' château in July, at the same time as John Leech and his wife, while Frank Stone and his family occupied a house on the Saint Omer Road.[5]

In October of the same year the long-projected journey to Switzerland and Italy actually took place, Augustus Egg being of the party. The story of it has been told many times in the story of Dickens' life, but of Collins we hear comparatively little. From Chamounix, Dickens wrote to say that the party had climbed to the Mer de Glace, and had then disorganised the hotel by demanding hot baths. It was on this trip that Egg was nearly swept away by a falling rock. Thence they went to Lausanne and visited Mr. Haldimand's Blind Institution, where they saw a deaf, dumb and blind youth in whom Dickens had taken an interest during a previous stay in Switzerland. Probably Collins profited by this to pick up information about deaf-mutes for the book he was then engaged upon, *Hide and Seek*. At Genoa, Egg and Collins are mentioned at having "gone out to kill the lions", while at Milan, Dickens is found approving of the temper of his fellow-travellers: "We continue to get on very well together. We really do admirably. I lose no opportunity of inculcating the lesson that it is of no use to be out of temper in travelling, and it is very seldom wanted for any of us."[6] The tribute was no doubt well earned; poor Egg had suffered a series of misfortunes, his shoes having been left behind by the courier in Paris and his dressing-gown at Domo d'Ossola, while for Collins, never an energetic man, the exertion of being remorselessly walked over the Simplon by the indefatigable Dickens must have been particularly trying. From Genoa an abominably crowded steamer took them to Naples: "Ladies on the tables, gentlemen under the tables, and ladies and gentlemen lying indiscriminately on the open deck, arrayed like spoons on a sideboard. No mattresses, no blankets, nothing. Towards midnight, attempts were made by means of an awning and flags to make this latter scene remotely approach an Australian encampment; and we three lay together on the bare planks covered with overcoats. We were all

---

[5]John Forster, *The Life of Charles Dickens,* ed. J. W. T. Ley (London: Cecil Palmer, 1928), pp. 594-595; *Charles Dickens as Editor,* p. 108.
[6]*Letters of Charles Dickens,* 2d edn. (London: Macmillan, 1893), p. 304.

gradually dozing off when a perfectly tropical rain fell, and in a moment drowned the whole ship. Thr rest of the night was passed upon the stairs, with an immense jumble of men and women. When anybody came up for any purpose we all fell down; and when anybody came down we all fell up again" (*Letters of Charles Dickens*, pp. 308-309). By Dickens' exertions, things were somewhat improved on the following night:

> The store-room down by the hold was opened for Egg and Collins, and they slept with the moist sugar, the cheese in cut, the spices, the cruets, the apples and pears — in a perfect chandler's shop; in company with what the _____'s would call a "hold gent" — who had been so horribly wet through overnight that his condition frightened the authorities — a cat, and the steward — who dozed in an armchair, and all night long fell headforemost, once in every five minutes, on Egg, who slept on the counter or dresser.   (Page 309)

Dickens himself had begged or borrowed another passenger's state-room and done the journey in solitary comfort. In this manner they got to Naples, where Collins was able to renew his memories of fifteen years before. They went up Vesuvius, and explored Herculaneum and Pompeii and then went on to Rome. At this point, Dickens mentions that the tale of their "losses" to date includes "two pairs of shoes (one mine and one Egg's), Collins' snuff-box, and Egg's dressing-gown", a reminder that Collins, like his father, was always an inveterate snuff-taker. From Rome, where Egg and Collins visited the Vatican Gallery, the party went on to Venice, and here Egg and Collins, who seem to have done most of the sightseeing together, are mentioned as being "out in a gondola with a 'servitore di piazza' " while Dickens stays behind in the hotel to write his letters and work on the Christmas number of *Household Words*. Thence they passed on to Florence, where Dickens observes: "The intolerable nonsense against which genteel taste and subserviency are afraid to rise in connection

---

[7]Forster, p. 586. [Miss Sayers has confused the itinerary in the text. The party went first to Florence, then to Venice. Dickens' observations seems clearly to have been written in Venice. He continues: "In the very same hour and minute there were scores of people falling into conventional raptures with that very poor Apollo, and passing over the most beautiful little figures and heads in the whole Vatican because they were not expressly set up to be worshipped. So in this place. There are pictures by Tintoretto in Venice more delightly and masterly than it is possible sufficiently to express. His Assembly of the Blest I do believe to be, take it all in all, the most wonderful and charming picture ever painted". Ed.]

with art, is astounding. Egg's honest amazement and consternation when he saw some of the most trumpeted things was what the Americans call a 'caution.' "[7] An article by Collins, expressing exactly this point of view, and entitled "To Think, or Be Thought For?" appeared in *Household Words* for September 13 and 20, 1856;[8] the two famous masterpieces chosen for special attack being Michael Angelo's "Last Judgment" in the Sistine Chapel and Raphael's "Transfiguration", which Egg and Collins had seen together when they visited the Vatican. The tone of militant common-sense, the confident appeal to "intelligent people in general" as against "learned authorities", and the rather irritating cocksureness which offends us in every paragraph are characteristic of the Victorian middle-class point of view which Dickens and Collins held in common.[9] This need not altogether blind us to the facts that much of the criticism is justified, and that Collins, after all, did know what he was talking about when he talked about painting; but it makes us wonder whether, perhaps, Dickens — whose taste in matters of art was unreliable — was quite the most broadening and catholic influence that might have been desirable for a young writer who still had much to learn.

The last town visited on this journey was Turin, whence the travellers returned home by way of Paris.

Back in London, Collins found his time well occupied by his work on the new novel and on *Household Words* and by his increasing intimacy with the Dickens circle. In March he is planning a trip to Rochester with Dickens; in April, an invitation to dine at Tavistock House is followed by the suggestion that he should join Dickens in Boulogne in the

---

[8]The article was a topical one, suggested by the purchase for the National Gallery of a Bellini, whose authenticity was in dispute among experts.

[9]The enormous and growing importance of the middle class was thoroughly appreciated by Collins from a practical point of view. He said to Holman Hunt on one occasion: "Of the English aristocracy the majority have no care for their country's art. The works of the old masters . . . which some of them collected, might all have been bought for English collections without advancing British art one whit. The men who really opened the way for you painters were the manufacturers when finding themselves rich enough to indulge in the refinements of life." And after pointing out that these patrons did not want "Jupiter, Venus, and Minerva" or ecclesiastical subjects, but works within their own intelligences and akin to their own interests, Collins added: "Those were the appreciators who founded English art, and they showed their good British common-sense. You artists and the whole country owe them a debt of gratitude for having done it" (*Pre-Raphaelitism*, I [New York: Macmillan, 1905] 310-311).

following summer (June to October) and "write the third volume of 'that' book there" (*Letters*, p. 17). Actually, *Hide and Seek* was completed ahead of schedule and published on June 6th 1854.[10]

In some ways, *Hide and Seek* is a less interesting and original book than *Basil*. It is a pleasant tale with a happy ending, full of golden hearted grotesques, such as Mat Marksman the rough American trapper, the deaf-mute "Madonna", Mrs. Peckover the clown's wife; even Valentine Blyth, the kindly little artist, is sometimes tiresome in his sentimentality. The whole story of the deaf-and-dumb child and her rescue from the brutal circus-manager has far too much of the conventional tearfulness of its period. The plot is not satisfactory. There is a "secret", and, so far, we may claim the book as the first "genuine Collins," but that secret is, in the words of Andrew Lang, "as well kept as it is absurdly discovered,"[11] and the discovery relies upon a series of coincidences so fantastically improbable as to shatter all belief. That the illegitimate daughter of the hero's father should happen to be adopted by the hero's best friend might perhaps be swallowed — such things may occur from time to time — but that the hero should then accidentally encounter in a music-hall the girl's maternal uncle, who has been scouring the country in the hope of finding and punishing his sister's seducer is an accumulation of coincidence that sticks in the gullet; and while we may believe that "Madonna's" resemblance to her dead mother was striking enough to establish her identity at first glance, we really protest against the identification of the seducer by the mere fact that his son's hair was of the same colour as that contained in a hair-bracelet belonging to the girl. Such evidence should not have been accepted by any author with a legal training. The hand of Collins the mystery-monger is still fumbling and uncertain.

These absurdities tend to blind the reader to the very real merits of the book. Dickens, writing to Miss Hogarth on 22nd July, observes:

---

[10] *Hide and Seek*. By W. Wilkie Collins, author of "Antonina," "Basil," &c. In Three Volumes. London: Richard Bentley, 1854.
[11] *Contemporary Review*, 57 (1890), 23.

> Neither you nor Catherine [Mrs. Dickens] did justice to Collins' book [*Hide and Seek*]. I think it far away the cleverest novel I have ever seen written by a new hand. It is in some respects masterly. Valentine Blyth is as original, and as well done, as anything can be. The scene where he shows his pictures is full of an admirable humor. Old Mat is admirably done. In short, I call it a very remarkable book, and have been very much surprised by its great merit. (*Letters*, p. 19)

In "doing" Valentine Blyth, Collins had, of course, his own personal experience of painters and their habits to draw upon. We recognise many little touches from the life of William Collins — such as the little jest of the pen and pencil painted on the threshold — and the account of the visitors at the "private view" is obviously authentic. We recognise the autocratic Lady Brambledown, with her genial bullying of painter and guests alike; the doctor, criticising the anatomy of the figures with the technical pedantry of the "Tailor and Cutter" sitting in judgment on the costumes of Academy portraits; and we are perfectly familiar with the

> two Royal Academicians — a saturnine Academician, swaddled in a voluminous cloak, who stared at the pictures with a speechless pertinacity which quietly annihilated them as works of art — and a benevolent Academician with an umbrella, who, not being able conscientiously to praise either "Columbus" or "The Golden Age," and being a great deal too fond of Valentine to blame them, compromised the matter by waving his hand vaguely before the pictures, and saying from time to time: "Yes, yes; ah! yes, yes, yes."

We also recognise the other types present: —

> There were M. Bullivant, the sculptor, and Mr. Hemlock, the journalist, exchanging solemnly that sort of critical small talk, in which words as "sensuous," "aesthetic," "objective," and "subjective," occupy prominent places, and out of which no man ever has succeeded, or ever will succeed, in extricating an idea. There was Mr. Gimble, fluently laudatory, with the whole alphabet of Art-Jargon at his fingers' ends, but with not the slightest vestige of comprehension of the subject, either in theory or practice. There were some respectable families who tried to understand the pictures, and could not. There were other respectable families who never tried at all, but confined themselves exclusively to the Dowager Countess .... And, finally, there was the absolute democracy, or downright low-life party among the spectators, represented for the time being, by Mr. Blyth's gardener, and Mr. Blyth's cook's father; who, standing together modestly outside the

> door, agreed in awe-struck whispers, that the "Golden Age" was a Tasty Thing, and "Columbus in sight of the New World," a Beautiful Piece.
>
> (II, 274-275)

There is genuine pathos in the story of the honest, though second-rate, artist, sacrificing his lofty ambitions in order to paint pot-boilers for the support of his invalid wife and adopted daughter. A bolder, and to modern minds more interesting conception, is that of the elder Zachary Thorpe. Having in his youth sown his wild oats and seduced (though with extenuating circumstances) a young woman who trusted him, he has developed into a sour Evangelical fanatic, grimly bullying his wife, and bringing up his only son in that very atmosphere of rigid seclusion from "the moral contaminations of the world" which had led to his own early escapade. The frightful atmosphere of Sabbatarian gloom in which the story opens is one of the most powerful pieces of writing Collins ever did, and we are in no way surprised that the younger Zack should turn out a rebellious youth, escaping nightly from home restraints to enjoy the society of prize-fighters and the dissipations of "theatres and public gardens — places of resort which Mr. Thorpe described, in a strain of devout allegory, as 'Devil's Houses' and 'Labyrinths of National Infamy'" (II, 42-43). To us, despite all allowance for his upbringing, young Zack appears (to quote Lang again) as "a rather drunken young rowdy, whom Mr. Collins fails to make amiable." Already, when Lang wrote in 1890, the manners of the young men of the day had become very much softened and civilised compared with what they had been thirty or forty years earlier. In *Basil,* Collins had enumerated Ralph's pursuits as a society man-about-town:

> he haunted the theatres, behind the scenes as well as before; entertained actors and actresses at Richmond; ascended in balloons at Vauxhall; went about with detective policemen, seeing life among pickpockets and housebreakers; belonged to a whist club, a supper club, a catch club, a boxing club, a pic-nic club, an amateur theatrical club ... (I, 58)

a list which, judging by contemporary records, errs on the side of respectability and refinement. In *Hide and Seek,* the "Snuggery", with its brandy-sodden, cigar-laden atmosphere, its lewd singers, bedizened trollops and insolent company is a true picture enough of the evening entertainment patronised by middle-class Londoners in the 'fifties, as may also be seen by Thackeray's description of the "Cave of Harmony" in *The Newcomes*. Nor were the upper classes much more particular about their amusements. Cock-fighting, rat-catching and the wrenching-off of bells and knockers were fashionable sports. The degraded condition of the Universities, exposed by the Royal Commission of 1850, had scarcely begun to alter for the better; scholarship had sunk to its lowest ebb, and the era of "clean sports" and muscular Christianity had scarcely dawned.[12] The intellectual and cosmopolitan aristocracy of the eighteenth century had given place to a more insular and barbarian aristocracy of wealth. The rise of industrialism, following upon the Reform Bill of 1832, had put power and prestige into the hands of the semi-educated; it had created a new word and a new thing — snobbery, and was giving a new and more alarming meaning to the word vulgarity. Dickens, with his amazing faculty for making vulgarity vital and lovable, bewitches us into enjoyment of scenes and people that, in actual life, we should find pretty intolerable: the coarse flavour of provincial life which is camouflaged in *Pickwick Papers* (1836) is pretty strong on the palate in *Handley Cross* (1843) and *Mr. Sponge's Sporting Tour* (1853).[13] In the novels of Thackeray, we can often only forgive the bumptious snobbery of the characters by preferring it to the contemptuous snobbery of the author; and the contemporary pages of *Punch* bear yet further witness to the general unpleasantness of the young man of the period. Never can there have been a time when such and so much impertinence passed muster for smartness, and those who to-day complain of the decline of courtesy and the

---

[12]"Of what strange doings were covered by the word 'sport', we may judge by the fact that after the University boat-race of 1862, both crews joined for the purpose of setting dogs on cats in a shed, the shed being provided by Cambridge and the animals by Oxford. As late as the sixties, it was a by no means unknown thing for a badger to be brought home, by some sporting young fellow, for the purpose of being torn from his tub, with merciless reiteration, by the teeth of terriers" (Esmé Wingfield-Stratford, *The Victorian Tragedy* [London: George Routledge and Sons, 1930], p. 260).

[13]A lady, observed Miss Mitford, might read "Pickwick" *aloud!* [The Miss Mitford in question was Mary Russell Mitford (1787-1855). In a letter to a Miss Jephson, she wrote in June 1837: "So you never heard of the *Pickwick Papers?* Well! . . . It is fun. London life — but without anything unpleasant; a lady might read it all *aloud*" (Constance Hill, *Mary Russell Mitford and Her Surroundings* [London: John Lane, The Bodley Head, 1920], p. 337). *Handley Cross* and *Mr. Sponge's Sporting Tour* are novels by Robert S. Surtees. Ed.]

boisterous behaviour of the Bright Young People would do well to study not only the great Victorian novelists, but the lesser men such as Albert Smith, Frank Smedley and Henry Cockton, before holding up the manners of the nineteenth century as a model for the twentieth.[14] Zack Thorpe, with his slang and his pugilism, is not a particularly attractive lad, for all his fundamental kind heartedness, but he is representative of his time and class.

A few autobiographical touches add to the interest the character has for us to-day. Zack's distaste for the tea-trade strikes a personal note:

> here I have been, for the last three weeks, at a Tea Broker's office in the city . . . . The governor and his friends say it's a good opening for me, and talk about the respectability of commercial pursuits. I don't want to be respectable, and I hate commercial pursuits . . . . Only fancy me going round tea warehouses in filthy Jewish places like St. Mary-Axe, to take samples, with a blue bag to carry them about in; and a dirty junior clerk who wears Blucher boots and cleans his pen in his hair, to teach me how to fold up parcels! (I, 92-93)

We should scarcely expect that Wilkie Collins, with his puny physique, was ever as much addicted as his hero to putting on the gloves, but he had at least some first-hand experience to help him when describing Zack's love of boxing and boxers, for he knew personally the greatest of all the bruisers. In later years, says R. C. Lehmann,

> he took our young imaginations captive with stories of Tom Sayers,[15] with whom he had often conversed, whose face-destroying hand he had shaken, whose awful arm he had felt. "He hadn't any muscle to speak of in his forearm," said Wilkie, "and there wasn't any show of biceps; but when I remarked on that, he asked me to observe his triceps and the muscle under his shoulder, and then I understood how he did it." (*Memories*, p. 29)

Autobiographical also is Zack's playful pretence (II, 103-104) of being desperately in love with Mrs. Peckover, a trait

---

[14]"Albert Smith describes a fine specimen of his type in the Jack Johnson of his novel *Mr. Ledbury* [1844] . . . . He is . . . what would nowadays pass for an unbelievable bounder, though in his creator's eyes he is obviously all that can be desired of a jolly, manly young Englishman" (Wingfield-Stratford, pp. 47-48).

[15]1826-1865. Sayers' great fight with Heenan, described by Thackeray in the *Roundabout Papers*, took place in [1860.]

borrowed from Millais, who carried on a perennial jest of the same kind with Mrs. Collins, and was always imploring the old lady to "name the day".[16]

And finally, is it possible to read the heart-rending account in Book II, Chapter 2 of Zack's return after a "thick night", without recognising the stamp of agonising inside knowledge? I understand from persons qualified to judge that nothing more vivid and convincing has ever been put on paper, and I am prepared to believe it. Here are not the pleasant humours of intoxication, such as accompanied Mr. Pickwick's excesses in the matter of cold punch — they are grisly realities, related with a cheerful absence of moral indignation which suggests that young Mr. Collins was a sad, dissipated fellow indeed!

The character of Old Mat, with his backwoodsman's habits and Red Indian instinct for finding his way about, would tell us, if we did not know it from other sources,[17] that Collins was a devoted reader of Fenimore Cooper. It is surprising that, this being so, he should have made the mistake of causing Mat to lose his scalp on the banks of the Amazon, which, as the trapper truthfully informs his young friend, is a South American river; possibly, after driving cattle in Mexico, exploring the overland route to the North Pole, catching wild horses on the Pampas and digging for gold in California, Mat had become as confused in his geography as Little Billee, who surveyed from his perch on the main-top-gallant:

> Jerusalem and Madagascar
> And North and South Amerikee![18]

Apart from this disconcerting inaccuracy, the character is pleasantly handled, though not with great originality.

---

[16]Ellis, pp. 22, 62. [W. Holman Hunt refers to this jest in *Pre-Raphaelitism*, I, 293. Ed.]

[17][In "Books Necessary for a Liberal Education," Collins concluded a series of unorthodox recommendations (for example, Dumas' "Monte Cristo") with this injunction: "Last, not least, do justice to a greater writer, shamefully neglected at the present time in England and America alike, who invented the sea-story, and created the immortal character of 'Leather Stocking.' Read 'The Pilot' and 'Jack Tier'; read 'The Deerslayer' and 'The Pathfinder,' and I believe you will be almost as grateful to Fenimore Cooper as I am" (*Pall Mall Gazette,* 11th February 1886, p. 2). In a letter to William Winter, dated 10th February 1882, Collins referred to Cooper as "that great Master (shamefully undervalued by Americans of the present day!)" and concluded: "N. B. I have just been reading 'The Deerslayer' for the *fifth* time." Winter included the letter in his volume of reminiscences, *Old Friends* (New York: Moffat, Yard, 1909), p. 211. Ed.]

[18][In Thackeray's ballad, "Little Billee." Ed.]

In making his heroine, "Madonna", a deaf-mute, Collins was led away, partly by the journalistic passion for "doing" something which had not been previously "done",[19] and partly by the curious fancy of the Victorian novelists for exploiting deformities and physical afflictions. It is true that such abnormalities afford an easy source of "sensation", pathos and horror, but it was not only the sensationalists who yielded to this temptation. Dickens, of course, had it badly: dwarfs, like Quilp and Miss Mowcher; cripples, like Jenny Wren and Tiny Tim; blind people, like Stagg and Bertha Plummer; mad men and eccentrics of all descriptions, from Barnaby Rudge to Miss Flite and Mr. Dick, from John Jasper and Mrs. Joe to Miss Havisham, work overtime to induce tears and shudders in the sensitive reader.[20] Reade made himself at home in the madhouse;[21] even Trollope deprived the Signora Neroni of the use of her legs for no very obvious cause.[22] Collins, in the course of his career, provided as shocking an array of physical and mental abnormalities as ever filled a case-book: starting off well with "Madonna", he thereafter tackled blindness in Leonard Frankland and Lucilla Finch, epilepsy in Oscar Dubourg, melancholia and facial disfigurement in Miss Dunross, spinal deformity in Rosanna Spearman, neurasthenia in Midwinter, atrophy of the limbs in Miserrimus Dexter, and assorted manias and imbeciles in Alfred Monkton, Anne Catherick, Jack Straw, Lady Montbarry, Simple Sally, Lewis Romayne and others "too numerous to mention".[23]

---

[19]"I do not know that any attempt has yet been made in English fiction to draw the characters of a 'Deaf-Mute,' simply and exactly after nature — or, in other words, to exhibit the peculiar effects produced by the loss of the senses of hearing and speaking on the disposition of the person so afflicted. The famous Fenella in Scott's 'Peveril of the Peak,' only *assumes* deafness and dumbness; and the whole family of dumb people on the stage have the remarkable faculty — so far as my experience goes — of always being able to hear what is said to them" (I, 296, Note to Ch. viii).

[20][[In the ms., Sayers left two blank spaces: "blind people, like _____"; and "from _____ to Miss Havisham." Only three blind persons appear in the Dickens canon, and Sampson Dibble, whom I do not use, appears only briefly in *The Uncommercial Traveller*. The structure of Sayers' sentence suggested no obvious candidates for the second blank, so I filled it with John Jasper, a dope addict, and Mrs. Joe, who had the sense as well as the meanness clubbed out of her. Quilp appears in *The Old Curiosity Shop;* Miss Mowcher, in *David Copperfield;* Jenny Wren, in *Our Mutual Friend;* Tiny Tim, in *A Christmas Carol;* Stagg, in *Barnaby Rudge;* Bertha Plummer, in *The Cricket on the Hearth;* Miss Flite, in *Bleak House;* Mr. Dick, in *David Copperfield;* John Jasper, in *Edwin Drood;* Mrs. Joe and Miss Havisham, in *Great Expectations*. Ed.]]

[21][[In *Hard Cash,* for example. Ed.]].

[22][[In *Barchester Towers.* Ed.]]

[23][[Frankland appears in *The Dead Secret;* Lucilla Finch and Oscar Dubourg, in *Poor Miss*

For the deaf-mutism of "Madonna" there is really little excuse, for it exercises no influence whatever on the plot and is a piece of pure virtuosity. It goes without saying that it has been carefully documented, and much stress is laid on the realism of the portrait — but at an essential point that realism stops short. Nothing is said of the painful irritability and unhappy suspicious temper which so often add to the burdens of the deaf. "Madonna" is represented as one of those models of angelic patience who are so tedious in fiction and, alas! so comparatively rare in real life. In this, Collins conformed to the convention that suffering refines the character. How else could he point the moral lesson of cheerfulness under affliction to which he is careful to draw attention in his footnote. The problem of evil is, as so often happens with preachers of morality, solved through being only partly stated. The timidity which overcame Collins here wrecked him, as it was to do again in *The New Magdalen* and again in *The Fallen Leaves,* and gave us a "Madonna" who is merely an embodied virtue — a conventional figure very unlike the magnificent heroines he was to create in the prime of his powers.

The one point in which *Hide and Seek* strikes a rather daring note for its period, or for any period, is in making "Madonna" fall in love with Zack Thorpe — her half-brother. But over this thin ice, Collins skates with the blandest unconcern, and since the discovery of the relationship automatically disposes of the infatuation, nothing remains to bring the slightest blush to the cheek of the young person.

The book, which is dedicated to Charles Dickens, had the misfortune to appear at the very moment of the outbreak of the Crimean War, and therefore attained no very great sale, though the demand "was just large enough to exhaust the first edition."[24] It added to his reputation, however, which it no doubt helped to redeem from the dreadful reputation of coarseness and impurity that *Basil* had earned for him. He was

---

Finch; Miss Dunross, in *The Two Destinies;* Rosanna Spearman, in *The Moonstone;* Midwinter, in *Armadale;* Miserrimus Dexter, in *The Law and the Lady;* Alfred Monkton, in *Mad Monkton;* Anne Catherick, in *The Woman in White;* Jack Straw, in *Jezebel's Daughter;* Lady Montbarry, in *The Haunted Hotel;* Simple Sally, in *The Fallen Leaves;* and Lewis Romayne, in *The Black Robe.* Ed.]

[24]Preface to 2d edn.

beginning to be "somebody", and even before the publication of *Hide and Seek* he is already established as a rising young man, whose recommendation of a friend's work to an editor is entitled to respect, as the following brisk little letter shows: —

> 17. Hanover Terrace, Regents Park
> May 3rd 1854
>
> My dear Sir,
> The Article which this letter accompanies has been written by a friend of mine now resident in Rome, and has been sent to me to be offered for publication in England. As it treats of a subject of some Art-interest, I take the liberty of sending it to the Editor of the Art-Journal. Will you oblige me by looking at it, and letting me know whether you think it can be rendered available for the pages over which you preside?
> In case you should not be able to make use of the Article, I will send for it to the Office, if you will order it to be left there with my name on it.
>
> I remain thus, My dear Sir,
> Very faithfully yours
> W. Wilkie Collins
>
> To Samuel Carter Hall Esqre.[25]

In July of 1854, Dickens, who was staying at the Villa du Camp de Droite at Boulogne, wrote to ask Collins to join him:

> I hope to finish [*Hard Times*] and get to town by next Wednesday night, the nineteenth; what do you say to coming back with me on the following Tuesday? The interval I propose to pass in a career of amiable dissipation and unbounded license in the metropolis. If you will come and breakfast with me about midnight — anywhere — any day, and go to bed no more until we fly to these pastoral retreats, I shall be delighted to have so vicious an associate.... I have met with what they call in the City "a parcel" of the celebrated 1846 champagne. It is a very fine wine, and calculated to do us good when weak.
> (*Letters of Charles Dickens*, p. 336)

On 30th July Collins was in Boulogne, but by the end of September was back again in England. During the remainder of this year he seems to have had no full-length novel in hand, but to have been occupied upon his tales and articles for *Household Words* and other papers. At Christmas, the Dickens

---

[25][Ms. of letter in H. R. C. Ed.]

household was absorbed in private theatricals for the children, and Collins joinèd in and took a part in *The Fairy Extravaganza of Fortunio and his Seven Gifted Servants* by Planché, "dozen words — but great Pantomime opportunities —" writes Dickens, "which requires a first-rate old stager to devour Property Loaves. Will you join the joke and do it? Gobbler, one of the seven gifted servants, is the Being 'to let.' There is an eligible opportunity of making up dreadfully greedy" (*Letters*, pp. 21-22). And lest this Bormacide feast should prove too tantalizing he adds persuasively that there will be "Pork, with sage and inions, at half past 5."

The performance, in which Dickens, Mark Leman and Collins, were the only adult actors, was a great success, and led to the idea of giving a "grown-up" play at Tavistock House. Collins was selected as the dramatist, and, taking the plot of *Gabriel's Marriage,* turned it into a melodrama, *The Lighthouse.* During the early part of the year he was at work upon this, and also upon the "long-short" story of *Sister Rose,* which was published in four parts in *Household Words,* beginning on April 7th. In an interesting letter dated 19 March, Dickens, after reading the first two parts of the story, makes a correct guess at the solution of the "secret" involved, and suggests how that secret might be better preserved (*Letters,* pp. 25-26); Collins seems to have taken his advice in part, at any rate. The story is a tale of the Terror, lively and dramatic in handling. It was published later as one of the stories in *After Dark.*

In February, Collins spent a week in Paris with Dickens. During this spring, his health seems again to have given him trouble. In the letter of 19 March above mentioned Dickens asks "How are you getting on? Shall you be up to a day at Ashford to-morrow week?" and on 24 March is "charmed to hear of the great improvement"; but about ten days later, Collins is still in the doctor's hands — apparently for some nasal trouble, since, on 4 April, Dickens hopes "the medical authorities will not . . . cut your nose off to be revenged on your face" (*Letters,* p. 30). On 15th April, however, Dickens writes again:

> Hurrah!
> I shall be charmed to see you once more in a Normal state, and

Dorothy L. Sayers

THE SMALLEST THEATRE IN THE WORLD!
TAVISTOCK HOUSE.

LESSEE AND MANAGER - - - MR. CRUMMLES.

On Tuesday Evening, June 19th, 1855, will be presented, AT EXACTLY EIGHT O'CLOCK,
AN ENTIRELY NEW AND ORIGINAL
DOMESTIC MELO-DRAMA, IN TWO ACTS, BY MR. WILKIE COLLINS,
NOW FIRST PERFORMED, CALLED

THE LIGHTHOUSE.
THE SCENERY PAINTED BY MR. STANFIELD, R.A.

AARON GURNOCK, *the head Light-keeper*	MR. CRUMMLES.
MARTIN GURNOCK, *his son; the second Light-keeper*	MR. WILKIE COLLINS.
JACOB DALE, *the third Light-keeper*	MR. MARK LEMON.
SAMUEL FURLEY, *a Pilot*	MR. AUGUSTUS EGG, A.R.A.

THE RELIEF OF LIGHT-KEEPERS, BY MR. CHARLES DICKENS, JUNIOR, MR. EDWARD HOGARTH, MR. ALFRED AINGER, and MR. WILLIAM WEBSTER.

THE SHIPWRECKED LADY	MISS HOGARTH.
PHŒBE	MISS DICKENS.

Who will sing a new Ballad, the Music by MR. LINLEY, the Words by MR. CRUMMLES, entitled

THE SONG OF THE WRECK.

I.
The wind blew high, the waters raved,
A Ship drove on the land,
A hundred human creatures saved,
Kneeled down upon the sand.
Three-score were drowned, three-score were thrown
Upon the black rocks wild ;
And thus among them left alone,
They found one helpless child.

II.
A Seaman rough, to shipwreck bred,
Stood out from all the rest,
And gently laid the lonely head
Upon his honest breast.
And trav'ling o'er the Desert wide,
It was a solemn joy
To see them, ever side by side,
The sailor and the boy.

III.
In famine, sickness, hunger, thirst,
The two were still but one,
Until the strong man drooped the first,
And felt his labours done.
Then to a trusty friend he spake—
" Across this Desert wide
" O take the poor boy for my sake ! "
And kissed the child, and died.

IV.
Toiling along in weary plight
Through heavy jungle-mire,
These two came later every night
To warm them at the fire,
Until the Captain said one day :
" O seaman good and kind,
" To save thyself now come away
" And leave the boy behind ! "

V.
The child was slumb'ring near the blaze :
" O Captain let him rest
" Until it sinks, when GOD's own ways
" Shall teach us what is best ! "
They watched the whiten'd ashey heap,
They touched the child in vain,
They did not leave him there asleep,
He never woke again.

HALF-AN-HOUR FOR REFRESHMENT.

TO CONCLUDE WITH
The Guild Amateur-Company's Farce, in One Act, by MR. CRUMMLES and MR. MARK LEMON;

MR. NIGHTINGALE'S DIARY.

MR. NIGHTINGALE	MR. FRANK STONE, A.R.A.
MR. GABBLEWIG, *of the Middle Temple*	
CHARLEY BIT, *a Boots*	
MR. POULTER, *a Pedestrian and Cold Water Drinker*	MR. CRUMMLES.
CAPTAIN BLOWER, *an Invalid*	
A RESPECTABLE FEMALE	
A DEAF SEXTON	
TIP, *Mr. Gabblewig's Tiger*	MR. AUGUSTUS EGG, A.R.A.
CHRISTOPHER, *a Charity Boy*	
SLAP, *Professionally Mr. Flormiville, a Country Actor*	
MR. TICKLE, *Inventor of the celebrated Compounds*	MR. MARK LEMON.
A VIRTUOUS YOUNG PERSON IN THE CONFIDENCE OF MARIA	
LITHERS, *Landlord of the Water Lily*	MR. WILKIE COLLINS.
ROSINA, *Mr. Nightingale's Niece*	MISS KATE DICKENS.
SUSAN, *her Maid*	MISS HOGARTH.

Composer and Director of the Music, Mr. FRANCESCO BERGER, who will Preside at the Piano-forte.
Costume Makers, MESSRS. NATHAN, of Titchbourne Street, Haymarket. Perruquier, MR. WILSON, of the Strand.
Machinery and Properties by MR. IRELAND, of the Theatre Royal, Adelphi.

DOORS OPEN AT HALF-PAST SEVEN. CARRIAGES MAY BE ORDERED AT A QUARTER-PAST ELEVEN.

DICKENS
PART III. No. 5

Playbill of *The Lighthouse.*
Courtesy of Humanities Research Center, Austin, Texas.

propose Friday next for our meeting at the Garrick, at a quarter before 5. We will then proceed to the Ship and Turtle. (*Letters,* p. 31)

Collins was a member of the Garrick Club till 1858, when he resigned, with Dickens, over the quarrel between Yates and Thackeray.

By 11th May, Collins had got the first draft ready for Dickens' inspection (*Letters,* p. 33). Dickens dealt with it in his usual prompt manner, making many alterations and writing in passages[26] and on 21 May was writing to Collins:

> Lemon assures me that the Parts and Prompt book are to arrive to-day. Why they have not been here two days I cannot for the life of me make out. In case they *do* come, there is a good deal in the way of clearing the ground that you and I may do before the first Rehearsal. Therefore, will you come and dine at 6 to-morrow (Friday) and give the evening to it? (*Letters,* p. 35)

On the previous day, he had written to Clarkson Stanfield the R. A., telling him about the "lark" in contemplation, and asking him to paint the scenery for the play. "We mean," he adds, "to burst on an astonished world with the melodrama, without any note of preparation. So don't say a syllable to Forster if you should happen to see him" (*Letters of Charles Dickens,* p. 368). (It was no doubt this kind of thing which annoyed Forster: why should Dickens have larks with Collins and he be left out of the conspiracy?) On the 23rd, Stanfield came to view the ground, and the next day is reported as being "bent on desperate effects, and all day long with his coat off, up to his eyes in distemper colours" (p. 369). Frank Stone was urged to come and play his original part in *Mr. Nightingale's Diary,* which was to conclude the performance: "You will find the words come back very quickly .... Katey and Georgina .... in wild excitement .... " And on the same day, Dickens informs Collins that he has "written a little ballad for Mary" (p. 370). With all this energy being expended all round, the preparations were rushed through in record time, and the performance took place on 19th June, Dickens (under the stage name of "Mr. Crummles") taking the leading part of Aaron Gurnock, Collins, that of his son Martin, Mark Lemon and Augustus Egg doing Jacob Dale and Samuel Furley, Georgina Hogarth appearing as the Lady and Mary Dickens as Phoebe.

---

[26]The ms. is in the Victoria and Albert Museum, and shows the work of both hands.

> Last night was perfectly wonderful!!!
>
> Such an audience! Such a brilliant success from first to last! .... Lemon and I [Dickens] did every conceivable absurdity, I think, in the farce; and they never left off laughing. At supper I proposed your [Stanfield's] health, which was drunk with nine times nine, and three cheers over. We then turned to at Scotch reels (having had no exercise), and danced in the maddest way until five this morning.
>
> It is as much as I can do to guide the pen. (Page 371)

A great night! Dickens, who was eagerly interested in getting Collins' play publicly performed by Benjamin Webster at the Adelphi, had sent cards for the performance to various newspapers thinking that this extra publicity would be of assistance in securing Webster's interest. In this immediate object he failed; but he succeeded in attracting the attention of the French critic Emile Forgues, who, in November 1855, wrote for the *Revue des Deux Mondes,* a long, sympathetic and, on the whole, very just appreciation of Wilkie Collins and his work in a series of *Etudes sur le Roman Anglais.*

An interesting passage in this article is the comparison drawn by Forgues between Collins and Balzac. We have already noticed the traces of French influence in *Basil;* Forgues finds them also in *Hide and Seek,* particularly in the character of Valentine Blyth, which he sets side by side with that of Pierre Grassou.

> Si nous comparons le type anglais au type français, nous trouverons le premier bien moins rigoureusement *fouillé,* analysé avec bien moins de curiosité patiente, une application, un acharnement bien moins grands. En revanche, grâce à l'humeur indulgente, à la tournure d'esprit essentiellement philanthropique qui caractérise ... M. Wilkie Collins, Valentin Blyth intéresse tout autrement que Pierre Grassou, et la compassion un peu dédaigneuse, mais sincère et cordiale, qu'on accorde au premier, ne ressemble en rien au mépris amer qu'inspire le second.[27]

Then comes a judgment which reads oddly, when we compare it with a later pronouncement by Andrew Lang:

---

[27][Sec. series, 12 (1855), 844: "If we compare the English type with the French, we shall find the first much less rigorously delineated, analysed with much less patient curiosity, with a diligence and relentlessness much less marked. On the other hand, thanks to the indulgent humor, to the essentially philanthropic cast of mind that characterises ... M. Wilkie Collins, Valentine Blyth interests us in an entirely different way than Pierre Grassou, and the compassion — admittedly a little disdainful, yet cordial and sincere — that one accords the first in no way resembles the bitter scorn inspired by the second." Ed.]

> Lui faut-il [i.e. à Collins] ... quelque profonde scélératesse à mettre en action, il en éprouve, dirait-on, un certain embarras, un certain remords. Il n'est à son aise et heureux d'écrire que lorsque ses personnages bien-aimés sont eux-mêmes dans toute la plénitude d'un complet bien-être.[28]

Thus Forgues in 1855; but in 1890 Lang, looking back over the whole of Collins' work, thought otherwise:

> We still find in him a man with an almost bitter sense of human unhappiness, a man whose favourite characters are at odds with the world. (Page 20)

Both critics were right. Collins in his heyday of youth, writing under the immediate stimulation of Dickens and in the first joy of finding his feet in a new world of pleasure and success, was a very different person from what he later became, after a life broken by ill-health and saddened by grief and disappointment.

Forgues concludes his article with a shrewd and necessary warning:

> Les chemins passablement ardus de la célébrité se sont aplanis pour lui. La critique le choie et le caresse. Les anciens du métier lui font amicablement « place dans le rang » sans attendre que le jeune et joyeux conscrit ait péniblement conquis tous ses chevrons. Charles Dickens, par exemple, réunissait, il y a quelques semaines, une brillante élite de spectateurs pour assister, chez lui, à la représentation d'un petit mélodrame ... L'heureux auteur qui débutait d'une façon si éclatante ... et dont la *maiden-play* était si vaillamment patronée par les premiers écrivains et les premiers artistes de son pays, qui donc était-il? On l'a déjà deviné. Au filleul de Wilkie, au fils de Collins, à l'heureux auteur de *Basil,* pareille bonne fortune était nécessairement réservée.[29]

Success too early and too easily won is dangerous. It

---

[28] [Page 844: "If required ... to set in motion some profound wickedness, one would say that he experiences a certain difficulty, a certain remorse. He is only at his ease and happy in writing when his beloved characters are themselves enjoying the abundance of a complete sense of well-being." Ed.]

[29] [Page 845: "The fairly steep paths to celebrity are smoothed out for him. Critics coddle and caress him. The veterans of the profession make room in the ranks for him without waiting for the young and joyous draftee to have laboriously won his stripes. Charles Dickens, for example, brought together a few weeks ago a brilliant elite to attend in his home the performance of a little melodrama .... The lucky author who made his debut in so dazzling a fashion ... and whose maiden-play was so spiritedly backed by the foremost writers and artists of his country — who, then, was he? Doubtless, you have already guessed. It was on the god-child of Wilkie, the son, so to speak, of Collins — the fortunate author of *Basil* — that such good fortune was necessarily bestowed." Ed.]

encourages a too-confident optimism, which extends from the man to his writing:

> Une conception ingénieuse le séduit et lui suffit trop vite. Un à-peu-près de caractère spirituellement indiqué, mais qu'il néglige d'accentuer, de particulariser assez; — une esquisse heureuse, effleurée du crayon, — un groupe artistement disposé, mais qui tient dans la composition générale ou trop ou trop peu de place, — il n'en faut pas davantage pour satisfaire son facile enthousiasme.³⁰

The novel demands more — profounder study, closer analysis. The critic expects from Collins something in the nature of the "Comédie Humaine" — a patient and thoughtful study of contemporary manners and character.

> Qui serait mieux placé que lui, par exemple, pour nous peindre la vie d'artiste en Angleterre et de notre temps? Qui pourrait mieux nous indiquer, dans ce qu'elles ont de plus délicat, les influences tantôt favorables, tantôt contraires, de ce patronage aristocratique, à l'ombre duquel tant de talens ont éclos et tant d'autres ont péri?³¹

As far as hard work and patience went, as far as careful subordination of the part to the whole went, Collins took this advice and profited by it; but his development was not to be in the least like anything that Forgues could possible have foreseen. He was not destined to be a Balzac; but he had, if a lower, yet a more original destiny to accomplish: he was to invent a new school of fiction.

In the meantime, Collins was still trying to place *The Lighthouse* with a London manager,³² had published *The*

---

³⁰[Page 847: "An ingenious conception misleads and satisfies him too easily. An approximation of character, wittily conceived, but negligently accentuated, insufficeintly particularised; a happily-conceived sketch, too lightly pencilled in; a group artistically conceived in itself but out of scale with the rest of the work — nothing more is needed to satisfy his facile enthusiasm." Ed.]

³¹[Page 848: "Who would be in a better position than he, for example, to paint for us the life of the artist in modern England? Who would be better able to point out to us their most delicate qualities, the influences — sometimes favorable, sometimes not — of the aristocratic patronage in whose shade some talents have bloomed and others have perished?" Ed.]

³²"Let me know what Wigan says. If he does not take the play, and readily too, I would recommend you not to offer it elsewhere. You have gained great reputation by it, have done your position a deal of good, and (as I think) stand so well with it, that it is a pity to engender the notion that you care to stand better" (Dickens to Collins, 17th July, 1855, *Letters of Charles Dickens*, p. 376). Alfred Wigan was the manager of the Olympic Theatre, but *The Lighthouse*, though it was eventually produced at the Olympic had to wait till Robson and Emden took over the management [in August 1857.] A performance of the play for charity had been given at the Campden House Theatre during 1855.

Yellow Mask in *Household Words* during July, and was considering collecting his various short stories into book form, besides collaborating with Dickens upon *The Holly-Tree Inn* for the *Household Words* Christmas number.[33] The story he wrote for this last was *The Ostler,* which subsequently appeared in *The Queen of Hearts* with the title *The Dream-Woman*. During the summer he paid a visit to Dickens at Folkestone.[34] In November, we find him negotiating, though without success, for a new edition of *Hide and Seek*.

> 17. Hanover Terrace
> Regents Park
> November 1st 1855
>
> Sir,
> The copyright of my last-published novel — "Hide And Seek" becomes my property after the 17th of the present month, and I am desirous of disposing of it for republication in a cheap form. Under these circumstances, I address myself to you to know whether you would feel inclined to treat for the book with a view to including it among the novels of the "Popular Library".
>
> I trust that my connection with literature may be considered a sufficient warrant for my writing to you without having procured a formal introduction.
>
> I am, Sir,
> Your obedient Servant
> W. Wilkie Collins
>
> To Thomas Hodgson Esqre[35]

No new edition of the book appeared till 1861, when it was issued in one volume by Sampson Low, with a frontispiece by John Gilbert.

Caetera desunt —

---

[33]"Of course the H. W. stories are at your disposition. At the office I will tell you the idea of the Christmas number, which will put you in train, I hope, for a story" (Dickens to Collins, 30th September 1855, *Letters of Charles Dickens*, p. 378).

[34]Dickens' invitation (*Letters of Charles Dickens*, p. 375) is for July 31st. Whether he went then or later is uncertain. On September 30th, Dickens writes as though he had just left them: "We missed you very much, and the Plorn was quite inconsolable" (p.378).

[35][Ms. of letter in H. R. C. Ed.]

MADONNA IN THE CLUTCHES OF THE BRUTAL CIRCUS MANAGER

APPENDIX

Among the mss. that Sayers collected and utilised in the preparation of her biography, the most interesting is the ms. of "Reminiscences of a Story-teller." This work was published in the *Universal Review* for 1888. This elegant journal was sponsored by Harry Quilter, a wealthy gentleman who greatly admired Collins' work. The ms., as Sayers notes, is vastly different from the published version. Since Collins often made extensive revisions in his galley-proofs, he may have been responsible for the changes. For purposes of this edition, I have been able to collate only the passage that Sayers actually quotes in Chapter II. I hope to publish a complete collation of the ms. and the published work later.

Material in italics appears in the ms., but not the published work; bracketed material, in the published work, but not in the ms. Unbracketed, unitalicized material is common to both.

Collation of Manuscript with Printed Version of "Reminiscences of a Story-Teller"

Renouncing, for these reasons, any attempt at a *sufficient treatment* [serious presentation] of the subject suggested to me, I think I see an alternative which permits me to gossip when I do not presume to instruct. What I might say in conversation with a friend can be said perhaps to many friends who *may* [will] open these pages. They may accept a little light talk growing out of casual recollections, if *I am lucky enough to amuse them — as condition which I am all the readier to respect, having first learnt to understand it when I was a boy at school. My first efforts in addressing an audience were made before a public of eight boys,* [they will kindly consent to be amused on easier conditions than I once encountered, when I was compelled to address my first audience] in the bedroom at school.[New ¶ in printed version] The *tallest, the strongest, and the* oldest *boy* [of the boys, appointed to preserve order,] was placed in authority over us, as captain of the room. He was as fond of hearing stories, *in bed,* [when he had retired for the night,] as the *oriental* [Oriental] despot to whose literary taste we are indebted for *the Arabian Nights*. ['The Arabian Nights';] *Our tyrant had exhausted the memories or the imagination as the case might be, of the other boys in his room when I joined the school. On the first night, my capacity in telling stories was tested at a preliminary examination — vanity urged me to do my best — and I paid the penalty. In other words,* [and] I was the unhappy boy chosen to amuse *the Captain from that time forth* [him]. It was useless to ask for mercy, and beg leave to go to sleep. In the event of my consenting to keep awake, and to do my best, I was warned beforehand to ['] be amusing if I wished to come out of it with comfort to myself.['] If I rebelled, the captain possessed *an instrument of correction* [a means of persuasion in the shape of (an improved *cat o' nine tails)* [cat-o'-ninetails] invented by himself. *He roused his satraps among the other boys and ordered me to be brought before him in words which I have never forgotten: "Bring Collins out to be thrashed."* When I was obstinate[,] I *took my thrashing* [felt the influence of persuasion]. When my better sense prevailed, I learnt, *in the presence of the instrument of correction, to make those calls on my invention which have been pretty often repeated in later years* [to be amusing on a short notice — and have derived benefit from those early lessons at a later period of my life]. Like other despots, the *Captain* [captain] had his intervals of generosity. *The most unwholesome things that I have ever eaten were gifts which rewarded me for telling a good story.* [; I owe to his system of rewarding me that 'passion for pastry' to which Byron tells us he was indebted for the privilege of reading Wordsworth's poetry.] In after years, I never had *the* [an] opportunity of reminding *him* [the captain] that I had served my apprenticeship to *fiction* [story-telling] under his superintendence. He went to India with good prospects; [,] and died, poor fellow, a few years only after he had left school.

DOROTHY L. SAYERS
WILKIE COLLINS
A CRITICAL AND BIOGRAPHICAL STUDY
WAS DESIGNED BY THOMAS DURNFORD
JOANNE JOYS AND SANDRA KEIL OF THE
UNIVERSITY OF TOLEDO PUBLICATIONS OFFICE
IT WAS SET IN 10 POINT SCHOOLBOOK BY
AMERICAN COMPOSITION OF TOLEDO, INC.
PRINTED IN SEPTEMBER 1977 ON 70 POUND
WARREN'S OLD STYLE BY
COMMERCIAL LITHOGRAPH, INC.
OF LIMA, OHIO
AND PUBLISHED BY THE FRIENDS OF THE
UNIVERSITY OF TOLEDO LIBRARIES
IN OCTOBER 1977 IN AN
EDITION OF 1000
NUMBERED
COPIES

THIS COPY NUMBER

446